OGL

P9-AEU-928

658.72
B 9739

THE AMERICAN KEIRETSU
A STRATEGIC WEAPON FOR GLOBAL COMPETITIVENESS

David N. Burt
Michael F. Doyle

BUSINESS ONE IRWIN
Homewood, Illinois 60430

POINT LOMA NAZARENE COLLEGE
Ryan Library
3900 Lomaland Drive, San Diego, CA 92106-2899

© David N. Burt and Michael F. Doyle, 1993

All rights reserved. No part of this publication may be
reproduced, stored in a retrieval system, or transmitted,
in any form or by any means, electronic, mechanical,
photocopying, recording, or otherwise, without the prior
written permission of the publisher.

This publication is designed to provide accurate and
authoritative information in regard to the subject matter
covered. It is sold with the understanding that neither the
author nor the publisher is engaged in rendering legal, accounting,
or other professional service. If legal advice or other expert
assistance is required, the service of a competent
professional person should be sought.

*From a Declaration of Principles jointly adopted by a Committee
of the American Bar Association and a Committee of Publishers.*

Sponsoring editor: Jean Marie Geracie
Project editor: Lynne Basler
Production manager: Irene H. Sotiroff
Art coordinator: Mark Malloy
Compositor: Precision Typographers
Typeface: 12/14 Palatino
Printer: Book Press, Inc.

Library of Congress Cataloging-in-Publication Data

Burt, David N.
   The American keiretsu : a strategic weapon for global
competitiveness / David N. Burt and Michael F. Doyle.
      p.   cm.
   Includes index.
   ISBN 1-55623-852-5
   1. Industrial procurement—United States—Management.   I. Doyle,
Michael F.   II. Title.
HD39.5.B85   1993
658′2—dc20   92-46913

Printed in the United States of America
1 2 3 4 5 6 7 8 9 0 BP 0 9 8 7 6 5 4 3

PREFACE

Several important economic drivers impact on today's business community: the globalization of world markets, the push toward niche marketing, velocity (time-based competition), quality-based competition, cost advantages, the geometric acceleration in new technology and new product offerings, and the relentless push toward high-volume manufacturing with lot sizes as small as one. These pressures demand a thorough reevaluation of an organization's approach to Supply Management.

Supply Management is a strategic weapon equal in power and importance to marketing and conversion. The American Keiretsu is an advanced strategic sourcing and Supply Management process. This process provides a sustainable competitive advantage through developing and managing a strategic approach to the firm's "upstream" supply system. The American Keiretsu combines the best of the Japanese Supply Management concepts with the best of American entrepreneurship, flexibility, market discipline, and technology to establish a strategic weapon that provides global competitive advantages in the areas of:

- Defect-free raw material, components, and finished products and services.
- Reduced time-to-market.
- Product cost advantages.
- Technology access and control.
- Reduction of business risks.

The American Keiretsu can be used by manufacturers,

the process and services industries, and enlightened governmental agencies and their suppliers. The advanced approach to Supply Management has two components: a strategic one and a tactical one. At a strategic level, Supply Management includes:

- The identification of threats and opportunities in the firm's supply environment.
- The development of component and commodity strategies.
- Active participation in the corporate or strategic business unit planning process.

At an operational level, Supply Management is the process of:

- Describing requirements to be furnished by external suppliers.
- Identifying attractive suppliers.
- Establishing and maintaining appropriate relations with the most appropriate suppliers.
- Minimizing cost in the upstream portion of the value chain and in the conversion of these purchased materials and services.
- Minimizing the risks of unanticipated cost increases and of production disruptions.

Many leading firms have implemented cross-functional teams to conduct these activities. Management is recognizing the importance of the multidiscipline or cross-functional team approach to important Supply Management actions, such as design and development, sourcing, negotiations, and management of buyer/seller relationships.

At many organizations, 50 percent of the quality problems originate with defects in incoming materials. These defects are the result of design, development, and sourcing weaknesses in the firm's Supply Management system. Incoming defects are all but eliminated through adoption of American Keiretsu-type (AKT) techniques.

The time required to progress from concept to customer—allowing a firm to be the first to market with a quality product or service—can be reduced 25 percent or more through the development and maintenance of AKT techniques.

Whether in process firms, manufacturing, or service industries, purchased materials frequently represent 60 percent and more of the cost of goods sold. AKT techniques hold the potential of reducing these costs by 10, 15, and even 20 percent.

With today's geometric growth in technology, it is not possible for any company to own all the technology it needs to produce the products and services to remain competitive. The interdependence in technology between customer and supplier must be a major consideration in the development of a firm's supply strategy. Carefully crafted AKT strategies and the resulting collaborative relationships address present and future technology needs required to keep the firm's value chain competitive.

The objective of supply risk management is to identify and reduce risks. The establishment and management of AKT techniques and collaborative relationships is an efficient and effective means of reducing risks in the outside supply world.

The combination of greatly improved quality goods and services, reductions in concept-to-customer and cycle times, reductions in the costs of goods sold as a result of lower purchase prices and conversion costs, improvements in access to the supply world's technology and innovations, and reductions in the risks inherent in the purchase of goods and services provides a strategic weapon that will greatly enhance the firm's competitiveness and, under most circumstances, market share.

The American Keiretsu shows you how to convert your present supply challenges into a strategic weapon that provides sustainable competitive advantage in today's global markets.

David N. Burt
Michael F. Doyle

ACKNOWLEDGMENTS

Many people and organizations have played a role in the development of the concepts described and discussed in this book.

The intellectual and experiential foundation for our work was laid over the past 40 years, in large part, by Charles Hinkle, George Zinke, and Ruben Zubrow of the University of Colorado; Norman Maier of the University of Michigan; Bob Davis, Gayton Germane, Bob Jaedicke, Lamar Lee, Jr., classmate, Steve Wheelwright, and Ed Zschau, all of Stanford University; Arlo Kunkel, Jack Marr, and Bill Nickles, colleagues from Ford Motor Company; and Bill Cordes and Keith Garber, then of Rockwell International.

Our friends and colleagues at the University of San Diego, including Deans James Burns and Gary Whitney; Elizabeth Arnold, Dennis Briscoe, Jim Caltrider, Ellen Cook, Seth Ellis, Greg Gazda, Phil Hunsaker, Bob Johnson, Brenda Konrad, Bob O'Neil, Tom Morris, Diane Pattison, Margaret Peters, Bill Soukup, and Chuck Teplitz; and Dean Don Jacobs, Sid Deshmukh, and Eitan Zemel of Northwestern University's Kellogg Graduate School have all contributed in many ways. We thank them.

Bob Galvin, then chairman of the board of Motorola, and Author Hughes, president of the University of San Diego, displayed vision and leadership in assigning Mr. Doyle as the Motorola Executive in Residence at the University of San Diego. Without their vision, this book would not exist.

The University of San Diego's Strategic Supply Management Forum and its many participants over the past seven years have contributed to our thinking. The members of the

Industrial Marketing and Purchasing Organization (IMP), especially the participants at the Milan (Italy), Uppsala (Sweden), and Lyon (France) conferences, have provided excellent insight into the role of networking in strategic Supply Management. Laurie Le Fevre and his colleagues at the Australian Department of Administrative Services and Bengt Barius, D.B.A., of Lulea University in Sweden, have helped provide global balance to our thinking.

Authors W. Edwards Deming, Charles H. Ferguson, Daniel T. Jones, Jordan D. Lewis, Robert Parker, Michael Porter, C. K. Prahalad, Daniel Roos, George Stalk, Jr., Lester Thurow, and James Womack, all of the United States, and John Carlisle, David Farmer, and Gary Hamel, of the United Kingdom, all have contributed to our views.

Professors Richard L. Pinkerton of CSU, Fresno, and Lee Budress of Portland State University have conducted extensive reviews of early manuscripts and have provided invaluable constructive criticism and input. The reviewers selected by our wonderful editor, Jean Geracie, at Business One, Irwin have provided valued input. They are: Henry Crouse (a management consultant); Craig L. Fields, Ph.D. (chairman and CEO, Micro Electronics and Computer Technology Corporation); and Philip H. Francis, Ph.D. (vice president and chief technical officer, Square D Company).

We especially want to recognize the contributions of Michael Holcomb, our computer graphic artist, for his assistance in the development and production of the illustrations used throughout the book. We thank Pat Johnson for her tireless, patient, and timely assistance with the manuscript.

Additionally, we thank Sharon Burt and Linda Doyle for their support during the project.

D.N.B.
M.F.D.

CONTENTS

CHAPTER 1

BENEFITS OF THE AMERICAN KEIRETSU[a]

The communitarian Japanese business firms' modes of play are quite different from those of the Anglo-Saxons, and their success is going to put enormous economic pressure on the rest of the industrial world to change.[1]

Lester Thurow

The American Keiretsu is an advanced strategic sourcing and Supply Management process. This process provides a sustainable competitive advantage through the development and management of a strategic approach to the firm's "upstream" supply system. This approach ensures a committed supply base that contributes quality, timeliness, technology advantages, and cost control. The American Keiretsu combines the best of the Japanese Supply Management concepts with the best of American entrepreneurship, flexibility, market discipline, and technology. The result is a highly efficient and focused supply structure that can be used as a strategic weapon to provide competitive advantage.

This weapon is equal in power and importance to marketing and conversion. Recognition of this by many of America's global competitors and a handful of progressive American

---

[a] The Japanese word *keiretsu* roughly translates into the English word *group*. A keiretsu is a large group of related companies that share common interests, common banks, and, typically, interlocking boards of directors and cross-equity-participation. These groups resemble cartels in that they tend to restrict sourcing and other business interactions to their group. The Japanese version of the *keiretsu* is described in greater detail in Chapter 2.

FIGURE 1–1
Corporate Strategy Model

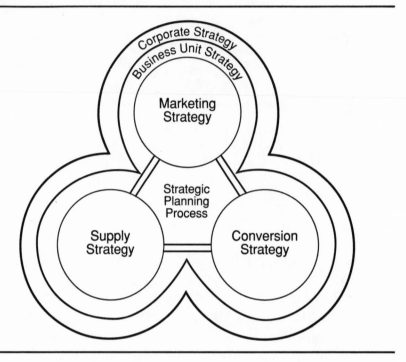

Source: Developed in cooperation with Charles L. Hinkle, Ph.D., University of Colorado.

firms gives them a significant competitive advantage. *The identification of threats and opportunities in the organization's supply environment must drive the development of appropriate strategic responses.*

The integration effort (illustrated in Figure 1–1) required to rationalize the supply strategy with the firm's corporate strategy must not be underestimated. The integration of supply, marketing, and conversion strategies is essential for survival and success in our emerging global economy.

The American Keiretsu is totally compatible with and is interdependent with several other cutting-edge approaches to modern management:

- Total quality management.
- Strategic cost management.
- Just-in-time.
- Simultaneous engineering.
- Flexible manufacturing.
- Core competencies.
- Value chain management.

Each of these approaches to management offers major competitive advantages. But they cannot be implemented without a strategic approach to Supply Management being in place! The concepts advanced in this book play a significant role in the success of each of these strategic managerial initiatives. In addition, Supply Management's leverage in the areas of cost, quality, velocity, and technology access make its early implementation essential to the success and survival of the firm.

THE KEIRETSU CONCEPT

The Japanese keiretsu has two components, horizontal and vertical. The horizontal keiretsu provides considerable control through equity ownership and efficient access to capital through its financial members. However, these horizontal activities have been sharply criticized by many American business and political leaders, and current U.S. antitrust laws preclude their adoption. The U.S. Federal Trade Commission is actively investigating Japan's automotive parts-buying habits in its two-year-old probe into possible antitrust violations.[2]

The vertical component of the Japanese keiretsu, however, contains important principles, many of which *are* adaptable to the American business environment. These principles recognize that constructive competition takes place between value chains and that competition within value chains is often dysfunctional.

The Japanese vertical keiretsu suffers from an inherent weakness—one which is the basis of superiority of its American counterpart: in Japan many first-, second-, third-, and fourth-tier suppliers are captives of their keiretsu masters. They are told what to do, how to do it, and how much they will be paid. In many cases, lower-tier suppliers are little more than sweatshops with only one customer and deplorable working conditions.

Members of an American Keiretsu, on the other hand, are driven both by competition and by their desire to grow their businesses profitably. These drivers create natural tensions to increase efficiency and to develop new technologies that increase sales volumes. Further, our prescription that any one manufacturer typically not represent more than 15 to 20 percent of its suppliers' business encourages suppliers to have important relationships with other customers, typically in other industries. These multiple relationships stimulate suppliers to be creative, innovative, and responsive. All parties gain from this cross fertilization and value-chain market orientation.

The American Keiretsu is responsible for the development, optimization, and management of both the internal and external components of the supply system. This represents the ultimate in Supply Management theory and practice.[b] The American Keiretsu provides the advantages of vertical integration without many of the well-documented disadvantages: span of control, transfer pricing issues, dilution of focus, and others.

This advanced form of Supply Management focuses on the integration and continuous improvement of two essential functions, each of which has historically been underrepresented as a value contributor. The first is the design, development, and implementation of a strategic approach to Supply

---

[b] It is interesting to note that the Malcolm Baldrige National Quality Award criteria promote closer supply chain alliances.

FIGURE 1–2
The Five Goals of Strategic Supply Management

Management (the strategic element). The second is the assessment, management, and effectiveness of the firm's Procurement Process,[c] from concept formulation through close-out of the supplier's invoice (the operational element).

As shown in Figure 1–2, strategic Supply Management plays a major role in satisfying the five basic objectives common to all successful business enterprises:

- **Quality:** the design, development, production, and delivery of defect-free products and services.
- **Velocity:** the use of time as a competitive weapon.
- **Cost Management:** the reduction of total cost resulting

[c]In an effort to minimize confusion, a number of terms, including procurement, Purchasing, Supply Management, and so forth, are defined in the following box.

BOX 1-1

Purchasing—The department that traditionally acquires materials and services from outside suppliers.

Procurement Process—The process of designing, specifying, sourcing, ordering, and disposing of materials, services, and equipment.

Supply Management—A new process responsible for the design, development, optimization, and management of both the internal and external components of the organization's supply system. At a strategic level, Supply Management includes: the identification of threats and opportunities in the firm's supply environment; the development of component and commodity strategies, including both inside manufacturing and outsourcing decisions; technology access and control; and active participation in the corporate or strategic business unit (SBU) planning process. At an operational level, Supply Management is the expanded process of: (*a*) identifying and describing requirements to be furnished by external suppliers, (*b*) identifying suppliers and establishing and maintaining appropriate relations with them, (*c*) measuring and optimizing cost in both the upstream portion of the value chain *and* in the conversion of these purchased materials and services into quality products, and (*d*) managing and measuring continuous improvement throughout the supply chain.

AKT (American Keiretsu-type)—AKT is used to describe a special type of relationship or alliance that emphasizes the critical nature of some upstream relationships. The expression describes an open relationship that meets the needs of both the buyer and the seller. Work is required to establish and to manage these relationships. AKT relationships are based on a large element of self-enlightened trust. AKT relationships or alliances normally are reserved for the procurement of critical materials and services, where the quality of the relationship is vital *to both parties.*

The term *AKT relationship* is used to meet two objectives: (1) to end the confusion involved in the use of the terms *supply*

BOX 1–1 (continued)

partner, partnership, and so forth. These terms have an array of meanings, ranging from the legal one, to an excuse to "bang the supplier over his or her head to lower the price," to truly collaborative ones, wherein the needs of both parties are met; (2) to simplify your reading. The alternative to the use of "AKT relationships" is "American Keiretsu-type relationships." We hope the use of this term improves readability.

World Class—A subjective phrase describing the quality of a buying or selling organization in all relevant areas, including Supply Management, technology, conversion, quality, cost management, and order and invoice processing. Due to the tendency of World Class organizations to improve continuously, the term *World Class* is an ever-moving target.

Throughout the text, these terms are capitalized since they have special meaning as defined and, therefore, are treated as proper nouns.

---

from the procurement and conversion of required materials and services.

- **Technology Access and Control:** the establishment and maintenance of technological advantage.
- **Risk Management:** the reduction of business risks inherent in the outside supply environment.

SUPPLY MANAGEMENT'S ROLE IN SATISFYING STRATEGIC OBJECTIVES

Several important economic drivers have an impact on today's business community: the globalization of world markets, the push toward niche marketing, velocity (time-based competition), quality-based competition, cost advantages, the geometric acceleration in new technology and new product offerings, and the relentless push toward high-volume manufacturing with lot sizes as small as one. These pressures demand a renewed and thorough evaluation of a firm's approach to Supply Management. (This system is portrayed in Figure 1–3.)

At a theoretical level, each sourcing and manufacturing step is a linked set of value-creating activities originating with Mother Earth, focusing on the end user, and returning to Mother Earth. (See Figure 1–4.) Truck tires are a good example of the complexity and potential of this level of strategic consideration. Several years ago, the Japanese decided to manufacture truck tires for domestic use. Large Japanese tire manufacturers sent representatives to America to see how truck tires were designed and manufactured. They found that America produced an 8-ply bias-belted tire for truck applications, which was 12-ply rated and which would carry 5,000

FIGURE 1–3
The Internal Supply Management System

FIGURE 1–4
The Value-Chain Concept

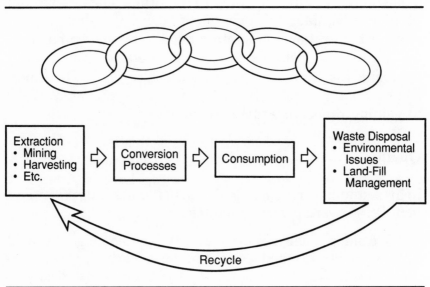

pounds. These tires could be recapped an average of one time. The Japanese decided to specify 14-ply truck tires for their domestic use. Obviously, 14-ply tires are far more expensive to produce than 8-ply tires, so why would otherwise intelligent engineers overdesign/specify truck tires to such an extent? The answer contains an example of the value-chain strategic thinking that is becoming so critical. The Japanese run their domestic tires until the tread is gone; then they sell the tire shells for around $75 to tire recappers in America. Fourteen-ply tire shells are in high demand as recaps. These tires can be recapped three or four times before they are sent into *America's* landfills.

The firm with the best-managed and most efficient Supply Management system for a given product or service realizes advantages that aid in meeting the five basic objectives of improved quality, velocity, cost management, technology, and risk management. Each of these five objectives, when implemented, offers significant leverage for the Supply Management system to contribute to the firm's sustainable competitive advantage. "Corporate perceptions that going it alone is better than cooperating need to be overcome, as do organizational obstacles to work cooperatively with other companies as a first, rather than as a last, resort."[3] The American Keiretsu provides the most scientific approach available to gaining this competitive advantage!

Quality

In his seminal work, *Quality, Productivity, and Competitive Position*, W. Edwards Deming writes:

> We are in a new economic age. We can no longer live with commonly accepted levels of mistakes, defects, material not suited to the job. . . . Acceptance of defective materials, poor workmanship, and inattentive and sullen service as a way of life in America is a roadblock to better quality and productivity. We have learned to live in a world of mistakes and defective products as if they were necessary to life. It is time to adopt a new religion in America.[4]

Quality is a critical value-chain issue. This means that the responsibility for quality extends from Mother Earth throughout all subsequent operations, *no matter what they are or where they are performed,* to the ultimate customer. It is this ultimate customer who will decide the success or failure of the value chain by buying a product or service from firm A, which feeds firm A's upstream value chain, or by buying a competitive product or service from firm B, which feeds firm B's upstream value chain. Revenue enters this system only when the ultimate customer buys a product or service. Transactions within the value chain simply pass portions of the ultimate customer's money along the chain.

Without costly inspection, re-work, and scrap programs, *companies cannot produce a better-quality product or service than the quality they receive from their suppliers!* Many companies attribute more than 50 percent of all their quality problems to purchased materials. Strategic Supply Management plays a key role obtaining quality products during the design, development, and sourcing of materials that are defect free. These materials, when integrated during production or used in service operations, result in quality products and services that have a high likelihood of success in the marketplace.[d] During design and development, quality is "designed in" by the firm's design team. This team *must* include design, process, and quality engineers; purchasing and marketing professionals; *and the firm's supply partners.*

Weaknesses in the Traditional Approach to the Design of Products

The traditional approach of relying on the firm's design engineers to perform all design functions and assume total responsibility for the quality, acceptability, producibility, reliability, and procurability of purchased materials and services is a major source of quality problems. For example, designers frequently develop requirements and specifications for materials and services to be furnished by outside suppliers with little or no regard for the suppliers' technical limitations or process capabilities. As a result, defects and variation in incoming materials and services occur. Often, these materials are the source of process yield losses, re-work, scrap, and defective products and services.

Today, World Class suppliers develop quality plans even as they prepare proposals on component designs. At the same time, these suppliers must develop specifications for

---

[d]"The Profit Impact of Marketing Strategy (PIMS) program is based on the experience of more than 450 companies in nearly 3,000 'businesses' for periods that range from two to twelve years. . . . Essentially, PIMS is a cross-sectional study of the strategic experience of profit organizations.

PIMS data show that in the long run, the most important single factor affecting a business unit's performance is the quality of its products and services relative to those of competitors."[5]

process and quality procedures, manufacturing and test equipment, and control software. World Class suppliers must achieve the desired level of quality *in the first article produced.*

The Role of Standardization
Quality is greatly enhanced when standardized materials are designed into the product or service. Hewlett-Packard has invested millions of dollars developing its catalog of standard components. These items are furnished by carefully prequalified suppliers. Hewlett-Packard design engineers are encouraged to specify such standard components. At many Hewlett-Packard divisions, specification of other than cataloged standard components requires the approval of the plant or division manager. The use of such standardized items has played a key role in Hewlett-Packard's tenfold reduction in incoming defects and lower costs and the enhancement of the quality of its products.

Selecting and Motivating the Right Source
Sourcing, the process of identifying and selecting suppliers with the capability and motivation to provide defect-free materials and services on time, plays an essential and an interdependent role in the firm's efforts to produce quality products and services. This interdependency is forced by the design and process engineering required to minimize variability. *Like design, sourcing is a team responsibility.* Sourcing is a crucial activity. As the late Lamar Lee of Stanford University often said, "Selection of the right source is the key to obtaining the right quality." "We learned one thing fast: you don't find quality suppliers—you make them."[6]

Howard and Shelly Gitlow, in their book *The Deming Guide to Quality and Competitive Position* write that a "Deming company" buys both a supplier's process and its products. The buying firm has to become involved in helping the supplier improve its processes over the long run. Such action requires a long-term perspective and a willingness to get involved in real change as opposed to purchasing for one time only, with no concern for future needs.[7]

Traditionally, purchasing authorities have advocated competitive bidding for selecting sources, provided certain essential prerequisites were satisfied. Unfortunately, competitive bidding is incapable of identifying suppliers offering optimal cost, quality, service, and technology. Today, an increasing number of supply teams use competitive negotiations with preselected sources of critical materials. This approach is used in large part to ensure that selected suppliers understand all aspects of the requirements (with an emphasis on quality), and have the process capability required to ensure success.

The Effect of Over-Emphasis on Price

Dr. Deming's fourth point or charge to management is *"End the practice of awarding business on price tag alone."*[8] Overemphasis on purchase price can have a direct (and disastrous) impact on quality and total cost management. The actions of buyers in the U.S. automotive industry in the early 1980s show the negative implications of focusing on price while ignoring other key issues. A 1982 *Business Week* article entitled "Detroit Is Trying Harder for Quality" indicated that "The automakers turn the screws to the point where it's almost impossible to make money selling to the auto companies. So the vendors have to make it (profit) on spare parts in the after market. That gives them a vested interest in failures, a miserable arrangement."[9] But now many buyers at selected Ford, GM, and Chrysler divisions focus on the *total* cost of purchased materials, with quality receiving its proper share of attention. These buyers are still hard bargainers concerned with reducing the cost of items, but some more enlightened buyers do this by motivating and assisting their suppliers to become more efficient. This increased efficiency is the source of lower *total* costs, with full recognition that quality must come first. Chrysler Corporation is making solid progress in the achievement of improved buyer–seller relations through this more enlightened approach. Chrysler Corporation saved over $3 billion in cost in 1991 alone as a result of numerous cooperative supply initiatives.[10]

Managing the Relationship

The Supply Management system's next area of responsibility for ensuring product and service quality is management of both the resulting contract and its relationships with suppliers. Unfortunately, this area receives altogether too little attention, frequently resulting in avoidable quality problems and late deliveries. Several key activities must take place to minimize the likelihood of quality problems at this point in the Supply Management process.

On critical procurements, Purchasing must bring key players from the buying firm and the supplier together to ensure that there is a complete understanding of all the specifications, along with the intended use, processes, and applications. In addition, it is frequently desirable to have operations, quality, and design engineering personnel visit the supplier's facilities to better understand these engineering operations and process requirements. Frequent visits by key supplier personnel to the buyer's plant help avoid quality problems, too. Such visits allow the supplier's team to see exactly how and when its product will be used and to discuss specific issues with people "on the line" using the materials under review.

Motivating Suppliers

Some organizations have implemented programs to stimulate their suppliers' commitment to quality through positive, ongoing communication and interaction. These programs include getting top executives from supplier companies actively involved in the establishment and measurement of quality goals. These commitments are consistently reinforced and successes are publicly recognized.

Certification programs play a critical role in motivating suppliers to meet quality needs. Polaroid certifies suppliers based on demonstrated success in shipping parts on time with no defects. During the initial trial stage, Polaroid inspects incoming parts or materials to ensure conformance. It monitors the production and quality systems of approved suppliers through computerized audits of suppliers' statistical process control (SPC) and variables data and checks the calibration of their test equipment.

Effective supplier management also means providing timely feedback to the firm's suppliers. Hewlett-Packard (HP) rates its suppliers quarterly, semiannually, and annually, depending on the sensitivity of the components. Ratings are based on technology, quality, responsiveness, dependability, and cost. HP provides its suppliers with immediate ratings relative to their competitors. Moreover, members of HP's commodity procurement strategy teams meet quarterly with key suppliers to discuss overall performance. Discussions usually focus on process yields, the desirability of revising specifications to lower unit costs, or ways of reducing lead times and paperwork.

Eliminating Quality Problems

Hewlett-Packard has a very aggressive program for confronting and eliminating quality problems as they occur. When a defect is identified, all divisions are informed with a quality alert; divisions are then prohibited from buying from the supplier until it proves its process is restored. If the supplier requires assistance, HP will make a sourcing engineer available to work with the supplier's team. But there are no further sales until a correction notice is issued.

Supply managers must adopt an aggressive approach to incoming quality defects. Instead of simply returning the defect for replacement or asking for credit (the typical response), managers demand the development and implementation of a formal corrective action plan to avoid a recurrence of the defect. Ford Motor Company's Eight Discipline Report (Figure 1–5) is a good example of the corrective action process. Many firms have adopted this formal approach because of its proven success.

FIGURE 1–5
Problem-Solving Disciplines

1. ORGANIZE A CROSS-FUNCTIONAL TEAM:
   Include experienced representatives from all activities that can help define the problem, define casual factors, implement corrective actions, verification, and/or prevention.
2. DESCRIBE THE PROBLEM (WHAT):
   Utilize all indicators to identify and quantify the problem as completely as possible in customer terms or symptoms.
3. DEFINE ROOT CAUSES (WHY):
   Ask the question, "Why," as many times as required to drive to a definition of the underlying root causes.
4. IMPLEMENT INTERIM CORRECTIVE ACTIONS:
   Take immediate action to contain the problem within the company and in the field.
5. IMPLEMENT PERMANENT CORRECTIVE ACTIONS:
   Eliminate root causes of the problem, design and implement control actions as applicable, correct errors already produced.
6. VERIFY EFFECTIVENESS OF ACTIONS:
   Measure effectiveness of actions identified in steps (4) and (5) in quantifiable terms.
7. PREVENT RECURRENCE:
   Modify management operating systems, practices, procedures, and/or processes to prevent recurrence of similar problems.
8. DOCUMENT EACH STEP IN WRITING:
   Disseminate the completed report throughout the company and the supply base to ensure maximum learning and realize related corrective actions.
9. CONGRATULATE THE TEAM:
   Recognize the cooperative contribution of all the team members.

Source: Adapted from Ford Motor Company's Eight Discipline Report.

In these and in many other more subtle ways, Supply Management plays the key role in ensuring a flow of defect-free products through the value chain to the firm's ultimate consumers.

Velocity

Until rather recently, velocity has been a largely overlooked strategic weapon. But its importance is becoming equal to that of quality. George Stalk, Jr., in his 1988 *Harvard Business Review* article writes that

> as a strategic weapon, time (velocity) is the equivalent of money, productivity, quality, even motivation. Managing time has enabled top Japanese companies not only to reduce their costs but also to offer broad product lines, over more market segments, and upgrade the technological sophistication of their products.[11]

In this article, Mr. Stalk recognizes Supply Management's role in reducing what he calls "time." In addition, Mr. Stalk continues by integrating the issues of velocity, technology, and innovation when he argues that

> the effects of this time-based advantage are devastating; quite simply, American companies are losing [their] leadership of technology and innovation—supposedly this country's source of long-term advantage. Unless U.S. companies reduce their new product development and introduction from 36-48 months to 12-18 months, Japanese manufacturers will easily out-innovate and outperform them.[12]

In a February 23, 1988, *Wall Street Journal* article "Manufacturers Strive to Slice Time Needed to Develop Products," the authors report:

> Quality in U.S. industry may be up and costs down, but American companies like Xerox are still getting sideswiped by foreign competitors who get new and improved products to market faster. The edge these competitors get from shorter

development cycles is dramatic: Not only can they charge a premium price for their exclusive products but also they can incorporate more up-to-date technology in their goods and respond faster to emerging market niches and changes in taste.[13]

Velocity combines two components: (1) compressed development time (time to market) and (2) reduced production cycle time. The two components of velocity provide a tremendous competitive advantage to firms that learn how to gain and employ them. Effective Supply Management has much to contribute to both components. For example, a recent survey of members of the American Management Association Purchasing Council indicated that new product development time could be reduced an estimated 25 percent through AKT relationships.

Time to Market
The Profit Impact on Marketing Strategy (PIMS) database shows a strong correlation between being the first to the market and eventual market share. (See Figure 1–6.) The data also show a strong correlation between market share and profit level. PIMS data indicate that a firm with a 7 percent

FIGURE 1–6
Impact of Velocity

Product development cycle time
—PIMS (Profit Impact on Marketing Strategy) Database
- Strong correlation between first to market and market share.
- Strong correlation between market share and profit level.

Market Share	Pretax ROI
7%	10.1%
8–14%	16.2%
15–22%	19.8%
23–26%	22.3%
36%	32.0%

market share will tend to enjoy a 10 percent return on investment, whereas a firm with an 8 to 14 percent market share typically realizes a 16 percent return on investment, and a firm with a 36 percent market share tends to enjoy a 32 percent ROI. Thus, early to market leads to increased market share, which leads to greater profits.[14] Further, as time is reduced, so are cost and risk.

Velocity is the acceleration of ideas and materials on a preplanned course to provide worthwhile and timely products and services that meet the needs of targeted customers. In order to achieve success with velocity, new and strategic approaches to Supply Management must be developed and embraced.

Considerable data have been published indicating that the Japanese keiretsu environment has been able to transform a design concept into a quality product in approximately 60 percent of the time required for most of their American competitors. Even though significant progress has been made in selected industries, much work remains to be done. Quite obviously, in order to regain and maintain market share, American firms *must* continue to improve this performance and reduce the time required to progress from concept to customer.

Xerox's 1980s Experience

The development and maintenance of collaborative relations with key suppliers is a necessary and indispensable element required to reduce development cycle time significantly. The well-documented experience of Xerox during the 1980s demonstrates the impact of Supply Management not only on development time, but also on cost and the quality of incoming materials.

In 1980, Xerox's Japanese competition was selling copiers for what it cost Xerox just to make comparable machines. Xerox's copier manufacturing costs exceeded those of its Japanese competition by 30 to 50 percent. Developing a new product cost Xerox twice as much and took *twice as long* as its Japanese competitors. By 1982, Xerox's share of worldwide copier revenue had shrunk to 41 percent, one half of what it had been in 1976.

At the time, Xerox engineers designed virtually all copier components. Purchased materials represented about 80 percent of total copier manufacturing costs. Suppliers built to Xerox prints and specs, frequently at excessive costs. The supplier base included over 5,000 companies.

Xerox responded. Management reduced its supplier base to 400. It trained these suppliers in statistical process control (SPC), statistical quality control (SQC), just-in-time (JIT) manufacturing, and total quality commitment (TQC). Under a program of continuous supplier involvement, it included suppliers in the design of new products, often substituting performance specifications for blueprints, in the expectation that suppliers could better design final parts they were to make themselves.

The new supply approach at Xerox was a key contributor to the improved climate of 1985. From 1981 to 1984, net product cost was reduced by close to 10 percent *per year*. Rejects of incoming materials were reduced by 93 percent. *New product development time and cost each were reduced by 50 percent. Production lead times were reduced 65 percent, from 52 weeks to 18 weeks.*[15] Clearly, Xerox's suppliers and its Supply Management process represent a significant competitive advantage.

Process Cycle Time

The second aspect of velocity is process cycle time. This is a measure of the total elapsed time from receipt of a customer order to actual delivery. Here, the issues are quality improvement, complexity reduction, customer service, and inventory containment, along with asset and capacity utilization. Considerable time and attention have been directed toward reducing process cycle time over the past several years.

Familiar improvement initiatives include just-in-time

scheduling methods (JIT), electronic data interchange (EDI), and dedicated, focused, and/or co-located manufacturing. There is little debate over the importance of reduced process cycle time or about the considerable savings available through these techniques. The debate is aggressively joined, however, when the discussion moves to implementation. Some executives argue that many JIT initiatives simply move inventory to the preceding level in the value chain, with little actual savings. Others argue that costs are actually increased by the complexity and multitude of incompatible EDI specifications imposed by aggressive customers. Clearly, the full potential of these important programs can only be realized through considered and thoughtful implementation procedures.

The outstanding accomplishments of Atlas Door Corporation, under the leadership of its founder, Mr. Joel Goldschein, demonstrate the importance of an effective Supply Management system, particularly in a small start-up firm. Over a 10-year period, the firm was able to grow at an annual rate 10 percent higher than its industry and earn pretax profits five times the industry average. This sterling performance has been directly attributed to the Supply Management system, which allowed Atlas Door to design, manufacture, and deliver customized industrial doors more quickly than competition. Mr. Goldschein's agreements and cooperative supplier relations were the backbone of Atlas Door's business plan and success.

The full strategic impact of the supplier selection and sourcing function snaps into focus when a firm attempts to implement velocity improvement initiatives that are a necessary component of time-based competition.

Cost Management

Cost has long been viewed as the basis of a zero sum game in dealings between buyers and sellers. A "win" for the buyer was a "loss" for the seller. While economic power in several industries frequently resulted in abuses of power by the buying firms, which resulted in profit squeezes and quality problems, more commonly, power resided with the supplier who had perfect knowledge of its costs. Accordingly, buyers were, all too frequently, overmatched and overpowered by their supply counterparts.

The 1990 book *Zero Base Pricing*™: *Achieving World Class Competitiveness through Reduced All-In-Costs* redressed this imbalance.[16] Finally, the buyer has techniques to understand the seller's costs as well as, *or better* than, the salesperson with whom he or she is dealing. *Zero Base Pricing*™ also introduced the concept of total or "all-in-costs" as portrayed in Figure 1–7. At last those involved in the Supply Management process have the conceptual tools to address the total cost associated with the procurement and conversion of materials! Savings of 10, 15, and 20 percent are common.

But our evolution is not complete. We must embrace strategic cost management. The ultimate goal must address the issue raised earlier: the entire value chain must be globally competitive![e] Instead of shifting costs and profits between suppliers and purchasers, the focus *must be* the reduction—or elimination—of costs from the value chain. In the vast majority of cases, this is best done through AKT partnerships, as discussed in Chapter 3.

Technology

Technology represents a rich opportunity for Supply Management improvement. Core competencies exist throughout the entire value chain. A 1992 survey of 70 members of cross-functional supply teams at 18 Midwest firms estimated that improved access to supplier technology could improve their firms' market share approximately 7 percent. But technology

---

[e]For insight into some of the accounting issues raised by this issue, see John Shank's article: "Strategic Cost Management: New Wine, or Just New Bottles?"[17]

FIGURE 1-7
The Total Cost of Materials and Services

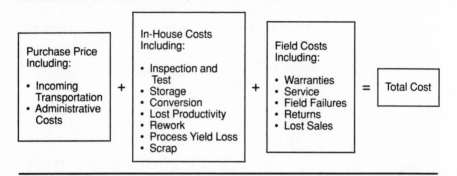

Source: Adapted from David N. Burt, Warren E. Norquist, and Jimmy Anklesaria, *Zero Base Pricing*™: *Achieving World Class Competitiveness through Reduced All-In-Costs* (Chicago, Ill.: Probus Publishing Company, 1990).

access is also the best-guarded and most difficult opportunity to realize. The guard standing at the door of the technology gold mine is the firm's own technology paradigm. This paradigm blocks ideas from "outside" and thereby prevents the early recognition and adoption of new concepts. Worse still is the failure of many firms to recognize or to fully utilize the technology, engineering, and R&D available within their own supply base.

With today's geometric growth in technology, it is not possible for any company on earth to "own" all of the technology that it needs to produce the products and services required to remain competitive. Deborah L. Wince-Smith, assistant secretary for Technology Policy, U.S. Department of Commerce, writes,

> Vertically integrated industrial entities can spread high R&D costs over a large product base and thereby reduce the financial exposure and risk in technology ventures. The involvement of multiple stakeholders activates the interdependency among upstream and downstream players in the technology "food chain." Players can mobilize resources quickly, pool

technical expertise, share long-term risks, and rapidly apply enabling technologies across a diverse product base.[18]

The technological interdependence between customer and supplier must be a major consideration in the development of the firm's supply strategy. Since product and technology life cycles continue to shorten, the supply strategy increases in importance and complexity.

Technology Development

Technology has a critical strategic dimension: to develop the required technology internally or to purchase it externally? In this age of technology expansion, many firms realize that it is simply not possible or affordable to develop all required technology internally. This realization drives difficult strategic choices about which technology to develop and "own" and which technology to purchase in the form of services, component parts, and assemblies. These strategic choices are not easy. The ramifications have far-reaching consequences. In any event, the firm *must* protect core technologies and processes, whether developed internally or acquired through carefully crafted strategic supplier agreements. At the same time, it must be cost competitive.

Technology Road Maps

Technology planning is one of the most important drivers in the strategic supply management planning process. It is not reasonable to manage a firm at a strategic level without a formal technology road map. Yet the vast majority of Western firms do not have a current technology road map. Those few firms that do seldom actively consider outside supplier technology as part of an interactive integrated strategic approach to the achievement of competitive advantage. Technology road maps take many forms. Each firm and industry must develop a model that is responsive to its unique circumstances. These models must also focus on appropriate technologies, including product technology, process technology, features, services, and so forth. During the early to mid 1980s, Professor Robert Kazanjian of the University of Michigan and Professor Robert Drazin of Columbia University conducted research on technology and innovation planning. They developed a basic technology planning approach that became the foundation of a popular University of Michigan executive seminar titled *The Strategic Management of Technology.*

The product evolution of the personal computer provides an example. Each new product offering in this fast-moving industry reduces the physical size of the product or increases its speed, memory capacity, and microcomputer function. The technology required for the next feature set improvement is often well known throughout this industry. This is the basis of a personal computer firm's technology road map.

Although the technology models and planning approaches may require customization based on the industry, the output goals remain constant. The basic idea is to identify, capture, and document those technologies, innovations, and/or enhancements that will drive the firm's future products. These identified technical issues are typically well known and occupy considerable focus within the engineering and marketing organizations. But in order to maximize technology leverage throughout the supply chain, this list must be discussed selectively with AKT suppliers. This process frequently becomes quite interactive. In effect, the original equipment manufacturer (OEM) or service firms and their AKT suppliers converge on the next generation of technologies. This process requires additional attention in many organizations.

Innovation
Innovation, technology's bedfellow, can play a major role in a firm's success. The history of innovation, however, appears to be random. When or where will the next innovation breakthrough occur? Based on the history of innovations, the only

certainty seems to be that the next innovation will occur where it is least expected.

Innovation is an important strategic objective. It involves both the internal and external environments. *Each value-added element or operation within the upstream value chain represents an innovation candidate.* This extends the traditional innovation horizon considerably and opens up many interesting additional sources of innovation. The problem is the random nature of innovation. Joel Barker, a noted futurist, has concluded that innovation *almost always* occurs outside the organization. He believes that an organization's own paradigm prevents people from innovating. This change appears to come full circle with no apparent resolution. For the most enlightened firms, the answer is to proactively monitor the external environment. Such monitoring is more than the marketing intelligence system that many firms currently employ. The process includes a system for innovation monitoring that actively looks at the upstream portion of the value chain and the supply base for each link in the chain. Innovation does not limit itself to marketing and engineering: the next major breakthrough may well involve a supplier. Strategic Supply Management must include an active plan to monitor, recognize, and implement innovative ideas available throughout the firm's supply system and even outside of the firm's present supply system.

"American suppliers, more than their Japanese counterparts, provide many of the advances that drive innovation. Elevate their role, and some executives believe that America can build an industrial system that is technologically stronger and swifter afoot than Japan's."[19]

Risk Reduction

The objective of risk management is to identify and reduce risks to an acceptable level. Some risks (those that can reasonably be anticipated) can be dealt with through the development of contingency plans. For example, an auto maker may source all seats for one model of car with supplier A, and all seats for another model with supplier B. Contingency plans call for both suppliers to be able to produce seats for both models for a reasonable period of time should either supplier become unavailable.

In addition to the reasonably anticipated risks inherent in quality, velocity, cost, and technology, two other areas must be addressed in a strategic Supply Management contingency plan: the risk of supply disruptions and the risk of significant unanticipated price increases.

The primary, but by no means only, way of dealing with these aspects of risk is through the establishment and management of AKT relationships. Much has been written on the pros and cons of these types of relationships. One thing is clear: carefully selected suppliers, carefully crafted agreements that incentivize both partners through good times and bad, and carefully managed AKT relationships with contingency plans significantly reduce risks in all of the areas discussed.

In the 1970s, Timex established close relationships with its key suppliers. In most instances, Timex established itself as a "preferred customer." During the two material shortages of the 70s, Timex's position as a preferred customer protected its continuity of supply. As more than one wit observed, "Timex never missed a beat due to supply disruptions."

Established, well-maintained AKT relationships also greatly reduce the likelihood of price shocks when compared with the traditional three-bids, spot-buy system. The organizations work together to control cost and price increases, as they share insight and data regarding the entire value chain that ultimately pays them both.

STRATEGIC SUPPLY MANAGEMENT ACTIVITIES

A major U.S.-based global manufacturer with activities in several core businesses recently invested some $7 million studying Japanese and European Supply Management actions. This highly successful firm obviously expects to gain a competitive advantage as a result of this investment.

Strategic Activities

These activities must ensure that the supply function is appropriately integrated within the corporate or strategic business unit (SBU) strategy. This match forces the SBU to focus on the timely and continuous availability of technology, materials, and services of the right quality at an acceptable total cost from its supply base. Strategic Supply Management activities must address the identification of threats and opportunities in the firm's supply environment, technology access and control, component and commodity strategies including both inside manufacturing and outsourcing decisions, the development and maintenance of appropriate information systems, the development of supply base and strategic alliance plans, and active participation in the corporate or SBU planning process. Strategic plans and activities frequently must consider options through several links of the supply system from the supplier's supplier at one end to environmental disposal and recycling strategies at the other end. Chapter 4 examines these complex concepts.

Operational Activities

Operational activities are responsible for the design, development, optimization, and management of both the internal and external components of the supply system. This crucial set of activities focuses on requirements planning and development, supplier selection, cost management, and management of supplier relationships. These activities are cross-functional in nature. Many leading firms have implemented cross-functional teams to conduct these activities. Management is recognizing the importance of the multidiscipline or cross-functional team approach to important Supply Management actions such as design and development, sourcing, negotiations, and management of buyer/seller relationships.

Supply base management activities also focus on how the firm interfaces with its present and potential suppliers. Typically, all or most of these relationships are experienced at the same time with different suppliers. These relationships are discussed in greater detail in Chapter 3.

MARKETING IMPLICATIONS

The concepts, techniques, and tools contained in this book can greatly enhance marketing's efforts to secure new markets and increase share in existing markets. Improved product quality, lower cost of goods sold, reduced time to market, and successful new products resulting from improved technology access to the firm's supply base combine to fulfill a marketer's wildest dreams of improved customer service and support.

Downstream Keiretsu-Type Partnerships

The proactive marketer will quickly recognize that AKT relationships may be initiated by either the buyer or, under selected circumstances, the seller. The seller must be sensitive to those limitations imposed in the United States by the Robinson-Pattman Act. Recently, during a supply system review of a major Midwest firm in a process industry, the director of marketing observed: "I'm going to start applying these ideas with several target clients. I'm confident that we can develop 'AKT relationships' with them. Wow!"

Professional buyers in an AKT environment demand that their key suppliers be open and cooperative in order for the buyer to understand all aspects of the supplier's operations impacting on the quality, cost, and timely availability of required materials and services. For example, the chairman of a supplier to the auto industry recently said, ''We've had to start sending finance types along with our sales engineers when calling on several accounts. The buyers want to know and understand everything about our processes and costs!''

Several proactive marketers are now going on the offensive: they are willing to share process and cost information with key customers. Since few of their competitors understand AKT relationships and the need for such openness, these proactive marketers are gaining a major competitive advantage!

Marketing executives are encouraged to study the concepts in this book. Chapter 10 advances several suggestions on how to apply many of these concepts.

APPLICABILITY

The American Keiretsu concepts are applicable to manufacturers, process and services industries, and to *enlightened* government agencies. The majority of examples cited are biased toward the procurement of direct materials. This is the result of two forces. First, most of the concepts and techniques outlined in the book were initially developed for the purchase of direct materials. Second, these Supply Management concepts are quite new and are only now starting to be applied to nonproduction and service procurement. There are considerably fewer examples of excellence to draw from; therefore, examples of outstanding practice, used for clarification through the book, tend to involve production materials.

The Supply Management concepts that will be introduced offer significant opportunities for the procurement of nonproduction and service requirements. The benefits outlined earlier in this chapter are just as real for indirect materials and services as they are for direct materials. The techniques, process improvements, and strategic approaches outlined are equally applicable to both categories of requirements and in general are directly transferable. The opportunity for developing AKT relations is similar to that for direct materials and is discussed in greater detail in Chapter 8.

Formal strategic supply management effectiveness initiatives have been underway for the past couple years at leading service and process industry firms including American President Lines, Ltd., Georgia Pacific, Canada Post, Pacific Bell, and Avery-Dennison. These initiatives normally are formally sponsored by the chief executive officer CEO or the Chief operating officer (COO) and/or Executive Committee and typically focus on *all* outside expenditures. These companies have been gaining significant efficiencies through aggressive approaches to Supply Management.

Cross-functional teams at these firms research and analyze past expenditure patterns. They review current and future requirements and develop formal strategic approaches that maximize the benefits of their spending. Opportunity areas include maintenance requirements, professional services, temporary labor, equipment and office leasing, capital equipment, construction, and inventory. Selected cost reductions ranging from 10 percent to 30 percent are being achieved routinely along with inventory reductions, improved service, better quality, and a marked improvement in office productivity.

A CAVEAT

Increasingly, executives and government officials are raising questions regarding U.S. antitrust laws. The recommendations contained in this book make sound business sense and have been approved for implementation by several firms. However, managers are encouraged to review their specific implementation initiatives with appropriate legal counsel.

THE IMPACT OF STRATEGIC SUPPLY MANAGEMENT

The self-assessment questionnaire (Figure 1–8) has been developed to provide an estimate of the likely impact of Supply Management initiatives at your firm. (You are encouraged to have Chapter 1 copied and distributed to your colleagues along with your request that the questionnaire be completed.)

PLAN OF THE BOOK

This chapter has introduced the principle that Supply Management makes contributions to the firm's success at both the strategic and operational levels and that Supply Management is equal in both power and importance to marketing and conversion.

Chapter 2 describes the Japanese keiretsu.

Chapter 3 describes the American Keiretsu in more detail and outlines the process of establishing an AKT relationship.

Chapter 4 addresses the eight dimensions of a supply strategy.

Chapter 5, "Bringing Quality Products to Market Quickly," overviews the impact of time on the product development and introduction processes.

In Chapter 6, the process of selecting the right source, whether internal or external, is discussed.

Chapter 7 explores the process of obtaining the lowest total cost associated with the ownership and conversion of purchased material.

Chapter 8, "NonProduction Requirements," addresses the contribution AKT relationships can play in the procurement of nonproduction requirements.

Chapter 9 examines the management of AKT relationships.

Chapter 10 describes how organizations across America

FIGURE 1-8
Self-Assessment Instrument

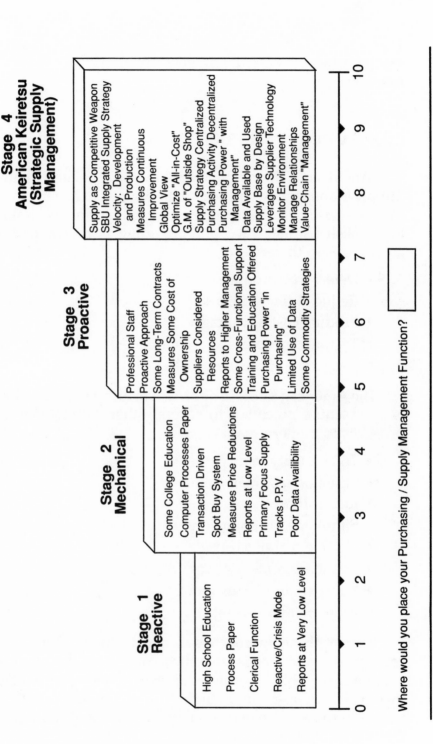

Where would you place your Purchasing / Supply Management Function?

can gain the benefits described throughout the American Keiretsu.

CONCLUDING REMARKS

The American Keiretsu combines the best of the Japanese Supply Management concepts with the best of American entrepreneurship, flexibility, market discipline, and technology to establish a strategic weapon providing global competitive advantages in the areas of:

- Defect-free products.
- Reduced time-to-market.
- Product cost advantages.
- Technology access and control.
- Reduction of business risks.

The American Keiretsu approach to Supply Management is an essential precursor to several other cutting-edge approaches to modern management:

- Total quality management.
- Strategic cost management.
- Just-in-time.
- Simultaneous engineering.
- Flexible manufacturing.
- The management of core competencies.
- Value-chain management.
- Agile manufacturing.

Each of these approaches to management offers major competitive advantages. But they cannot be implemented successfully without a strategic approach to Supply Management being in place. In addition, Supply Management's leverage in the areas of cost, quality, velocity, and technology access makes its early implementation essential to the success and survival of the firm.

Embracing strategic Supply Management and the development of AKT relationships will greatly enhance *your* competitiveness in the coming economic battles between the major trading blocks as described in Lester Thurow's recent book, *Head to Head.*[20] *The American Keiretsu* outlines a key prerequisite to success in these battles.

The American Keiretsu shows you how to convert your present supply challenges into a strategic weapon that will enhance your survival and competitiveness!

NOTES

1. Lester Thurow, *Head to Head* (New York: Alfred Morrow and Company, 1992), p. 114.
2. "FTC Hits Japanese Auto Group with Subpoena," *Automotive News* (March 9, 1992), p. 6.
3. 21st Century Manufacturing Enterprise Strategy (Bethlehem, PA: Iacocca Institute, Lehigh University, 1991), p. 9.
4. W. Edwards Deming, *Quality, Productivity, and Competitive Position* (Cambridge, MA: MIT, Center for Advanced Engineering, 1982), p. 19.
5. Subhash C. Jain, "Profit Impact of Market Strategy," *Market Planning & Strategy*, 3rd ed. (Cincinnati, OH: South-Western Publishing Company, 1987), pp. 356–360. The interested reader is also referred to Robert D. Buzzell and Bradley T. Gale, *The PIMS Principles: Linking Strategy to Performance* (Free Press).
6. Tom Peters, cited in *Made in the USA* by Roger L. Hale, Ronald E. Kowal, Donald D. Carlton, and Tim K. Sehnert (Minneapolis, MN: The Tennant Company, 1991), p. 7.
7. Howard S. Gitlow and Shelly J. Gitlow, *The Deming Guide to Quality and Competitive Position* (Englewood Cliffs, NJ: Prentice Hall, Inc., 1987), p. 58.
8. Deming, *Quality, Productivity, and Competitive Position*, pp. 7, 23.

9. "Detroit Is Trying Harder for Quality," *Business Week* (November 1, 1982), special report.

10. February 1992 personal interviews with Chrysler purchasing management.

11. George Stalk, Jr., "Time—The Next Source of Competitive Advantage," *Harvard Business Review* (July–August, 1988), p. 41.

12. *Ibid.*, p. 49.

13. John Bussey and Douglas R. Sease, "Manufacturers Strive to Slice Time Needed to Develop Products," *Wall Street Journal* (February 23, 1988), p. 9C.

14. Jain, "Product Impact of Market Strategy," p. 356.

15. David N. Burt, "Managing Suppliers up to Speed," *Harvard Business Review* (July–August, 1989), pp. 127–135.

16. David N. Burt, Warren E. Norquist, and Jimmy Anklesaria, *Zero Base Pricing*™: *Achieving World Class Competitiveness through Reduced All-In-Costs* (Chicago, IL: Probus Publishing Company, 1990).

17. John K. Shank, "Strategic Cost Management: New Wine, or Just New Bottles?" *Journal of Management Accounting Research* (Fall 1989), pp. 47–65.

18. A. Peisl, J. Aoi, D. L. Wince-Smith, M. B. Smith et al., "Can a Keiretsu Work in America," *Harvard Business Review* 68, no. 5 (September–October, 1990), p. 182.

19. "Learning from Japan," *Business Week* (January 27, 1992), p. 54.

20. Thurow, *Head to Head*.

CHAPTER 2

THE JAPANESE KEIRETSU

The superpower military warfare of the twentieth century will be replaced by economic warfare in the twenty-first century, and Japan will be the winner of the twenty-first century's economic wars.[1]

Shintaro Ishihara

The Japanese keiretsu is receiving increasing attention, study, and criticism in the West. Over the past three or four years, a growing number of diverse groups—executives, government leaders, U.S. congressional committees, *Business Week* magazine (January 17, 1992, and February 10, 1992), and even U.S. presidential candidates—have criticized the *Japanese* keiretsu. Most of these individuals have openly cited the Japanese keiretsu as a major reason for America's current economic ills. Lester Thurow takes a much more studied approach in his book, *Head to Head*. He sees a far more fundamental issue: "The British-American form of capitalism facing off against the communitarian German and (Nationalistic) Japanese variants of capitalism."[2] One thing seems abundantly clear: the intensification of global competition has only begun. This global competition will change the way America conducts business at a fundamental level. In the April 26, 1992, issue of the *Los Angeles Times*, David Friedman, a lawyer specializing in Pacific Basin business matters, wrote:

> Certain characteristics of Japan's equity markets, including the consolidation of stock by Japan's ubiquitous business groups, or *keiretsu*, make it possible for Japan to export much of the pain caused by the [1989–1992] Nikkei nose-dive. Most,

if not all, of the firms that make up the Nikkei 225 index are members of *keiretsu* groups—Mitsubishi, Toyota or Sumitomo, for example. Close to 70 percent of their outstanding stock is cross-held by other group members. These joint holdings are rarely, if ever, traded; they are locked away for protection against corporate control battles and to cement long-term relationships among affiliates.

Japan's largest firms and shareholders are thus relatively unaffected by dramatic declines in Tokyo stock prices because they never sell the bulk of their holdings. When *keiretsu* firms dabble in the market, they use their influence to hedge their bets. Scores of Japan's blue-chip companies, for instance, recently obtained covert investment guarantees from the four major Japanese brokerages, in effect compelling smaller and foreign investors to insure their profits.

Put another way, Japan's domestic equity market is primarily structured to preserve Japanese control of the country's major companies. Unlike in Europe and the United States, it is a marginal source of capital.[3]

In his 1988 book, *The Misunderstood Miracle*, David Friedman outlines three theories for Japan's economic success. He discounts the bureaucratic regulation theory and the market regulation theory as unsupportable by evidence. Mr. Friedman explains Japan's economic success as "primarily the result of greater diffusion of flexible manufacturing strategies." We have considerable difficulty with many of Mr. Friedman's findings, as do other researchers. In fact, Mr. Friedman appears to apologize for the Japanese system from time to time. Therefore, his finding, which follows, is most interesting:

> From 1956 to 1971 the (machine tool) industry was subject to the temporary measures for the promotion of the Machinery Industry Law, which authorized MITI to plan, set up cartels, and use incentives to promote selected industries. The Law was extended three times. After it finally expired, a new bill was passed, the Temporary Measures Law for the Advancement of Designated Electrical and Machinery Industries, which was in force from 1971 to 1978. This law, which listed

machine tools as one of its targets, again provided MITI with a panoply of powers to promote various industries. Finally, in 1978, the Temporary Measures for the Promotion of Information Machinery Law was passed. The bill's language tempered MITI powers of regulation, because of trade friction, but once again the law was designed to promote special equipment, and among the targets it listed were NC machines.[4]

This finding has led many to conclude that MITI, supplier cartels, and import restrictions have much to do with Japan's economic success.

BACKGROUND

In 1936, the imperial government of Japan selected Toyota and Nissan to produce trucks for the military. Both firms were in the textile and loom manufacturing business at the time. The two companies were instructed to develop their own parts suppliers within Japan. They were officially directed by the government not to purchase imported parts. Three years later, in 1939, the imperial government of Japan ordered Ford Motor Company and General Motors Corporation to close their Japanese manufacturing operations in Japan and to leave the country.

After the war, the Japanese economy was in ruins, resources were scarce, and capital investment was critically short. In order to reconstruct the economy, the government had to focus the nation's limited capital and resources on a few basic industries. The nation could not afford the luxury of duplication or excess capacity in its fledgling supply base structures. Additionally, the Zaibatsu cartel industrial structure, which was prevalent throughout Japan, was outlawed immediately after the war. The Zaibatsu structure was seen as an imperialistic holdover and a direct violation to free trade and accepted American antitrust concepts. These conditions spawned the development of the keiretsu, as the "legal" successor to the Zaibatsu. The Japanese keiretsu groups hold frequent meetings to plot strategy in their domestic and foreign markets. Such action would violate American antitrust laws.[5]

Structure

The Japanese keiretsu system combines horizontal scale, diversified production of related systems, vertical technical coordination, and market discipline. Each sector—particularly critical components and capital equipment—is concentrated but not monopolistic, thus guaranteeing stability and scale while preserving internal rivalry. Each company's production is partly but not wholly captive. Because products are dependent on the market, they are also disciplined by it—unlike wholly captive operations in vertically integrated U.S. companies, which often become complacent.

At the same time, Japanese producers have access to stable capital flows through both their parent companies and their banks. Thus they can absorb short-term losses and engage in comparatively risky long-term R&D, thereby insulating themselves from the short-term financial pressures that plague U.S. companies.[6]

Keiretsu members cooperate, buy from and sell to each other, share technology and R&D efforts, and have common financial institutions. This tight cooperation and coordination provides great advantage when competing with other manufacturers.

Japanese companies partition activities and then exchange results. They engage first in predatory pricing to eliminate rivals and then in cartelistic behavior to gain higher profits. They avoid excess rivalry in interaction with foreign competitors. They never poach each other's employees, and they buy preferentially from each other instead of from foreign or outside suppliers.[7]

Considerable data regarding the automotive keiretsu have been made available over the past 15 years by selected

Japanese and U.S. organizations. In order to better understand the Japanese keiretsu, the auto industry will be used as an example. All other keiretsu, which involve every major industry in Japan, work in very much the same way.

Figure 2-1, a model of a keiretsu system, was developed by Mitsubishi Research Institute, Inc., in 1987. This model is instructive and reflects the relationships of primary subcontractors with secondary suppliers. This pyramid structure is developed through formalized strategic supplier selection, not through competitive bidding or some other activity that would produce random results. It is interesting to note that the *strategic* selection of suppliers was a common concept in Japan prior to 1945. Only recently is the concept receiving limited attention in the United States!

As shown in Figure 2-1, the first-tier supplier is supported by a team of second-tier suppliers, third-tier suppliers, and possibly fourth-tier suppliers. These are "independent" group member companies that specialize in specific activities. These suppliers, at all levels, are not selected on the basis of competitive bids or competitive negotiations, but rather on the basis of relationships, performance, and group membership. The selection process is further influenced by the extensive cross-ownership of suppliers at various levels, which generally exists. Holding 5 or 10 percent or more of a supplier's equity is common in Japan.

Figure 2-2 provides a more specific frame of reference. The three examples in Figure 2-2 show the electronic component keiretsu for Toyota, Nissan, and Honda, as structured in 1987. Honda claims not to have a keiretsu. It calls its supplier "Kai" or "family," but by all accounts, the system works much the same way.

Keiretsu organizations are normally headed by large financial institutions. These banks and/or insurance companies see to the capital needs of the group. The next tier includes a major manufacturer (in these examples, large auto companies). The third tier contains primary system subcon-

FIGURE 2–1
Japanese Keiretsu Structure

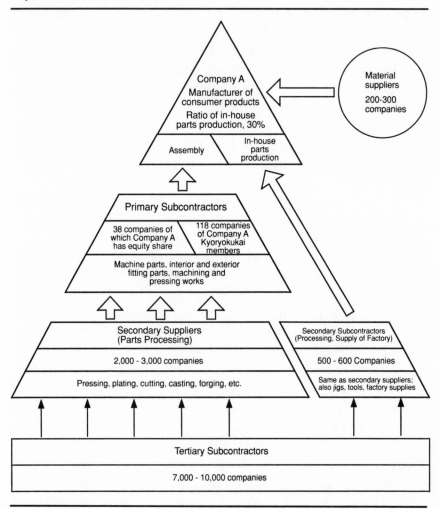

Source: Mitsubishi Research Institute Inc., "Relationship between Japanese Auto and Auto Parts Makers," February 6, 1987, p. 5. Reprinted courtesy of Japan Automobile Manufacturers Association.

tractors. The fourth tier contains parts or component suppliers.

Figure 2–3 contains a listing of the JAMA (Japan Automotive Manufacturers Association) keiretsu groups. These data

FIGURE 2–2
Selected Japanese Automotive Supply Structures

Mitsui Bank

Tokai Bank

Sanwa Bank

Toyota

Nippon Denso (TE)
Air conditioning
Electronic power control
Electrical parts

Fujitsu - Ten (TE)
Audio EFI

Fujitsu

Matsushita Tsuko
Comm system

Alshin Seiki (TE)
Transmissions

Aisan - Warner
Auto transmissions

Aisan (TE)
Carburetor

Matsushita

TE = Toyota Equity   Toshiba   Fujitsu   Matsushita   Hitachi

Tokyo Kaijko Kasai Hoken

Mitsubishi Shintaku Bank

Mitsubishi Bank

Honda

Denshi geken (HE)
ECU, cruise control

Showa Seisaku - Sho (HE)
Suspension control

Nishin Kogyo (HE)
Anti-skid

Matsushita Tsushin

Yazaki Keiki
Wiring

Nippon Denso
Electronic modules

Nihon Seiki (HE)
Dash

HE = Honda Equity   OKI   Matsushita   Nec   Toshiba

Dai-Ichi Seimei Hoken

Nihon Kogyo Bank

Fuji Bank

Nissan

JECS (NE)
Injectors, EEC
Power steering

Kanto Seiki (NE)
Sus control
Dash/drive comp

Nihon Jidohensoku (NE)
Transmissions

Jidosha Denki (NE)
Actuators

Nyles - Parts (NE)
Auto drive system

Hitachi Sawa
EEC, Anti-skid
sensors

Nihon Kikaki
Carburetor

NE = Nisson Equity   Hitachi   Toshiba   Mitsubishi

FIGURE 2–3
List of Automotive Keiretsu Groups

Auto Company	Name of Association	As of	No. of Members
JAPIA (Japan Auto Parts Industries Association)		Jan. 1989	426
Daihatsu Motor Co., Ltd.	KYOYUKAI	Dec. 1988	169
Fuji Heavy Industries Ltd.	YUHIKAI	July 1988	201
Hino Motors, Ltd.	KYORYOKUKAI	Dec. 1988	237
Honda Motor Co., Ltd.	(No association)	Dec. 1988	311
Isuzu Motors Ltd.	KYOWAKAI	Nov. 1988	285
Mazda Motor Corp.	YOKOKAI	Dec. 1988	179
Mitsubishi Motors Corp.	KASHIWAKAI	May 1988	353
Nissan Diesel Motor Co., Ltd.	YAYOIKAI	Jan. 1989	62
	SHINWAKAI	Jan. 1989	87
Nissan Motor Co., Ltd.	TAKARAKAI	Oct. 1988	104
	SHOHOKAI	June 1988	60
Suzuki Motor Co., Ltd.	KYODOKUMIAI	Oct. 1988	97
Toyota Motor Corp.	KYOHOKAI	Dec. 1988	176
	EIHOKAI	Dec. 1988	70
Total number of companies			1927

Source: September 1988 Fourin, Inc., "The Japan Auto Part Industries 1989/1990 Report." Reprinted with permission from Fourin, Inc., Nagoya City, Japan.

were developed and distributed by International Industries Institute, Inc., a Japanese research group headquartered in Negoya. This chart shows the auto firm on the left and the number of keiretsu members on the right. Each auto firm's keiretsu group has been formally named. As an example, the 346 members of the Mitsubishi Motors Corp. keiretsu are called Kashiwakai. (To many Americans, it seems amazing that a group of suppliers would be so structured that they would take or accept a formal name identifying them as formal members of a supply organization.)

Figure 2–4 lists a small sample of the type of formalized data that have been made available in English. These data were developed and distributed by International Institute, Inc. This sample is provided to show, in some detail, the extent of Japanese keiretsu relationships, which include "main bankers" and formal "keiretsu group membership." This is not the type of information that is typically provided in U.S. industrial association literature, and it speaks volumes about the formalized structure of the Japanese keiretsu.

The April 1990 issue of *Business Tokyo* provides additional important insights. According to *Business Tokyo* and recent Japanese government statistics, there are over 700,000 companies in Japan's nonprimary industry. Of these, only 0.7 percent have 300 or more employees; the other 99.3 percent are classified as "small- and medium-size enterprises." These small- and medium-size firms account for approximately 99.5 percent of all manufacturing in Japan. More than 56 percent of these firms are official keiretsu subcontractors working directly for a large parent company.[8] "At the pyramid's bottom is a swarm of job shops and family ventures with primitive working conditions and subsistence-level pay and profits."[9]

In a 1988 survey, large firms were asked by MITI (Ministry of International Trade and Industry) why parent companies use subcontractors. The overwhelming reply was to reduce cost. MITI did not ask why costs were reduced through subcontracting or how these lower costs were achieved. This MITI data did not show what subcontractors call *rieki kanri* (profit control). *Rieki kanri* is the ability of the parent company to control completely a supplier's operations, even to the extent of telling him to accept huge losses in order to maintain favorable pricing to the parent firm.

FIGURE 2–4
Published Data Sample

Name of Company	LST	Directors	Head Office	Main Bankers	④ Estblsmt ⑤ Capital ⑥ N. Emp
Abo Packing Seisakusho		Shohei Abe / pr.	1020 Hikawa Ato. Koshikitani, Ageo City, Saitama Pre. 352.	Mitsubishi Bank	④ Dec. 1953 ⑤ 10 ⑥ 75
Achilless Corp.	★	M. Tonooka / pr. S. Nakajima / vp. T. Suzuki / ex dr.	22 Daikiyo-cho. Shinjuku-ku. Tokyo	Fuji Bank Ltd. Ashikaga Bank Ltd. Taiyo Kobe Bank Ltd.	④ May 1947 ⑤ 13,282 ⑥ 2,776
Aichi Kiki KK		T. Yoshimura / ch. M. Kaneko / pr. T. Kijima / m drt.	3-4-14 Bitobashi Nakagawa-ku, Nagoya-City	Daishi Bank Ltd. Nagoya Sogo Bk Takai Bank Ltd	④ Jan. 1955 ⑤ 194 ⑥ 504
Aichi Leather Industry		Hisashi Ito / pr.	2-17-20 Tabata, Kita-ku Nagoya-city, Aichi Pre.	Tokai Bank Ltd Nagoya Sogo Bk Hachijuni Bk	④ Jan. 1957 ⑤ 30 ⑥ 230
Aichi Machine Industry Co. Ltd.	★	G. Utsuno / pr. G. Yokoiwa / vp.	2-20 Kawanami-cho, Atsuta-ku Nagoya-City, Aichi Pre.	Chuo Trust & Bk Fuji Bank Ltd. Ogakj Kyoritsu Bk	④ May 1949 ⑤ 3,895 ⑥ 4,403
Aichi Sharyo Co. Ltd.	★	S. Suzuki / pr. H. Sudo / vp. A. Yazawa / vp.	Nagoya Tsushi Bldg. 2-15-18 Chiyoda-ku Nagoya-City, Aishi Pre.	Tokai Bank Ltd Sanwa Bank Ltd Industrial Bank	④ Feb. 1962 ⑤ 2,303 ⑥ 630
Aichi Steel Works, Ltd.	★	M. Amano / pr. K. Arai / vp. T. Kato / ex drt.	1 Wanowari, Arao-cho Tokai City, Aichi Pre.	Tokai Bank Ltd Mitsui Bank Ltd. Sanwa Bank Ltd	④ Mar. 1940 ⑤ 14,640 ⑥ 3,485
Aiei Sangyo KK		Eiichi Aiba / pr.	2-4-32 Kita-Niiho, Sanjo-City, Niigata Pre.	Daishi Bank, Ltd.	④ Nov. 1944 ⑤ 140 ⑥ 107
Aiko Co., Ltd.		H. Iwamura / pr. T. Kondo / e mg dr.	6824, Nakatsu, Aikawwa-cho Aido-gun Kanagawa Pre. 243-03	Bk of Yokohama Taiyo Kobe Bank Shoko Chukin Bk	④ Jul. 1948 ⑤ 30 ⑥ 120
Aikoku Kogyo Co. Ltd.		Seiji Hishida / pr. M. Hishida / ex dr. H. Watanbe / m d.	11-1 Morigami-bongo Sobue-cho, Nakajima-Gun Aichi Pre.	Tokai Bank Ltd Chuo Trust & Bk Industrial Bk Japa	④ Aug. 1943 ⑤ 760 ⑥ 666
Aisan Industry Co. Ltd.	★	T. Kobayashi / ch. H. Takahashi / pr. T. Ando / vp.	1-1-1 Kyowa-cho. Obu-City, Aichi Pre.	Tokai Bank Ltd Mitsui Bank Ltd Sanwa Bank Ltd	④ Dec. 1938 ⑤ 3,247 ⑥ 3,031
Aisin AW Co., Ltd.		M. Nishimura / ch. S. Moronto / pr. N. Kasuva / v. pr.	10 Takane, Fujii-cho, Anjo-city, Aichi Pre. 444-11	Mitsui Bank Ltd Tokai Bank Ltd Sanwa Bank Ltd	④ May 1969 ⑤ 3,240 ⑥ 2,800
Aisin Chemical Co., Ltd.		H. Miyachi / pr. T. Kanakawa / v p. T. Kimura / e m d.	1141-1 Okawagahara. Iino, Fujioka, Nishikamo-gun, Aichi Pre. 470-04	Tokai Bank Ltd Mitsui Bank Ltd Sanwa Bank Ltd	④ Feb. 1952 ⑤ 715 ⑥ 685
Aisin Light Metal KK		M. Inaba / pr.	12-3 Nagonoe, Shinminato-City, Toyama Pre. 934	Tokai Bank Ltd Sanwa Bank Ltd Mitsui Bank Ltd	④ Feb. 1970 ⑤ 750 ⑥ 768

⑦ Sales / ⑧ Nt. Profit / Date	Main Products or Product Lines	JPA	DM	FH	HI	HM	IM	M	MZ	MT	ND	NM	SM	TM
⑦ 1.100 / ⑧ 10 / Sep. '87	gasket, gasket kits, press (stamping) works										X			
⑦ 88,647 / ⑧ 5885 / Oct. '87	headress, dashboards, seat, vinyl products synthetic leather													
⑦ 13,312 / ⑧ 45 / Sep ' 87	engines, transmission parts, machine works					X								
⑦ 7,800 / ⑧ 97 / Dec. '87	interior parts, leather products, boots, dust covers, grips, handle covers	★												X
⑦ 209,491 / ⑧ 2,638 / Mar. '87	engines, transmissions, production of automobiles (Nissan)											X		
⑦ 25,205 / ⑧ 2,636 / Mar. '87	production of special purpose vehicles													
⑦ 142,297 / ⑧ 3,395 / Dec. '87	rear-axle shaft, crank shaft, ring gears, differential ring gears, forging products.		X			X	X							X
⑦ 1,907 / ⑧ 169 / Dec. '87	oil pan, pulley, head-rest										X			
⑦ 2,369 / ⑧ 13 / Dec. '85	transmission/engine parts,						X							
⑦ 9,371 / ⑧ 85 / Feb. '87	transmission/engine parts, free balance arms	★			X					X				
⑦ 62,350 / ⑧ 2,318 / Mar. '87	carburetors, engine valves, synchronizer rings, throttle bodies, fuel pumps	★	X						X	X				X
⑦ 159,700 / ⑧ 9,894 / Dec. '87	automatic transmissions	★						X		X				X
⑦ 20,417 / ⑧ 1,174 / Oct. '87	paints, binding agents, tapes, moulding agents, friction materials	★												X
⑦ 18,205 / ⑧ 702 / Mar. '87	aluminium die-casting products alumina metal pattern forging products, alumina extrusion / forging parts													X

Source: September 1988 Fourin, Inc., "The Japan Auto Part Industries 1989/1990 Report," Reprinted with permission from: Fourin, Inc. Nagoya City, Japan.

There are numerous and considerable economic advantages of these pyramidal sourcing alliances. For example, the capital expenditure for the parts industry is concentrated within a relatively small number of supplier firms. This closed supplier structure reduces the amount of capital required by increasing equipment utilization within the industry in total, and it significantly improves the return on capital as compared with the American open-supplier structure. The dark side of this closed supplier structure was highlighted recently by Mr. Boone Pickens in a letter to the editor of *Business Week* in the February 17, 1992, issue. Mr. Pickens said in part:

> The rewards of the keiretsu are great—for those Japanese businessmen fortunate enough to sit in the gabled boardrooms of Tokyo. The reality for most Japanese individuals, however, is something totally different.
>
> In Japan, there are no such things as shareholder rights, consumer rights, or worker rights. There is no way, if you are a young Japanese individual, to start a business of your own, except perhaps for a hot dog stand. The keiretsu system is more akin to corporate communism than capitalism.[10]

HOW JAPANESE KEIRETSU SYSTEMS WORK

There are 11 automobile manufacturers and about 2,665 first-tier keiretsu suppliers, as previously shown in Figure 2–3. This number of suppliers is in contrast to the 8,000 first-tier suppliers of direct materials at General Motors, which currently maintains business relationships with approximately 30,000 suppliers. It is interesting to note that a counterpart Japanese automotive manufacturer may well have a similar number of suppliers in its upstream value chain; however, it maintains active business relations with fewer than 1,000 suppliers.

The pyramid supply structure of the Japanese keiretsu offers considerable competitive advantage in scale, volume, capital concentration, inventory efficiency, quality focus, technology concentration, and so forth. As a simple example of the competitive potential available in administrative cost alone, data have been developed reflecting the typical administrative burden associated with increased supply base complexity. This is depicted in Figure 2–5, "Invoice Activity Data."

In 1990, a U.S. firm, typical for its size and industry, received 200,000 invoices from approximately 8,500 suppliers. Less than 1 percent of the suppliers generated 25 percent of the total invoices. The reader should compare this with the Japanese keiretsu pyramid system, in which the issuance of invoice, receivers, and purchase orders has been eliminated for the most part.

Figure 2–5 portrays invoice activity by supplier for the same U.S. firm. It shows that a relatively small number of suppliers generate multiple invoices each working day. Two suppliers generate more than 10 invoices per day and 140 suppliers generate at least one invoice per working day. This complexity issue alone may answer some of the questions about why white-collar productivity in America is up only 4 percent over the past 20 years, while blue-collar productivity is up over 83 percent.

The above data address administrative complexity and Japan's advantage in this area. But this is only the tip of the iceberg: far more is going on in these keiretsu relationships. The following hypothetical example is offered in an effort to describe the Japanese keiretsu design, sourcing, and manufacturing process.

An Example

Suppose Toyota Management has approved the development of a new vehicle. Among many other things, Toyota needs a new starter motor for this project. Unlike Ford and General Motors, Toyota does not have a starter motor engineering staff. Its keiretsu partner, NipponDenso, has a starter motor design staff, since starter motors are one of its businesses. Toyota immediately contacts NipponDenso when the

FIGURE 2–5
Invoice Activity Data

a. Typical U.S. Firm Supplier/Invoice Curve (1990 Activity)

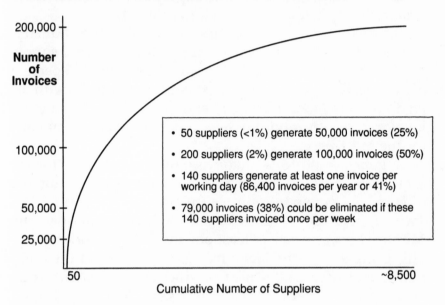

- 50 suppliers (<1%) generate 50,000 invoices (25%)
- 200 suppliers (2%) generate 100,000 invoices (50%)
- 140 suppliers generate at least one invoice per working day (86,400 invoices per year or 41%)
- 79,000 invoices (38%) could be eliminated if these 140 suppliers invoiced once per week

Cumulative Number of Suppliers

b. Invoice Activity by Supplier

Number of Invoices per Year	≥240	≥480	≥960	≥1440	≥1920	≥2400	Total
Average Invoices per Day	≥1	≥2	≥4	≥6	≥8	≥10	2.57 Average
Number of Suppliers in Category	78	38	12	6	4	2	140
Number of Invoices in Category	26,200	23,300	16,000	6,500	8,400	6,000	86,400

project is approved. Quite possibly, NipponDenso has an engineer assigned to and working in the Toyota design center. Toyota provides NipponDenso with its operational vehicle-level specifications, program timing information, and project financial data, including the target price to be used for the starter motor in the design-to-cost buildup.

This system focuses on getting cost out of the product during the planning and design stage. Its salient elements are depicted in Figure 2-6. The individuals involved are not simply accountants. They are senior-level cost engineers with broad experience in manufacturing, quality, engineering, and Purchasing.[11]

It should be noted that core technologies—those that the

FIGURE 2-6
Design-to-Cost Flow Example

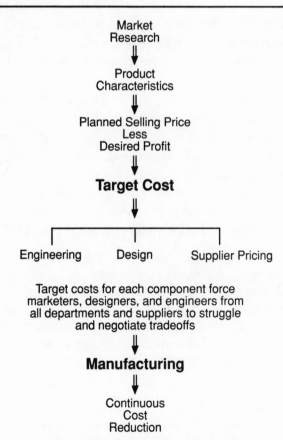

Market
Research
⇓
Product
Characteristics
⇓
Planned Selling Price
Less
Desired Profit
⇓
Target Cost
⇓

Engineering   Design   Supplier Pricing

Target costs for each component force
marketers, designers, and engineers from
all departments and suppliers to struggle
and negotiate tradeoffs
⇓
Manufacturing
⇓
Continuous
Cost
Reduction

assembler firm feels provide it a competitive advantage—generally are developed in-house. Engines, transmissions, major body panels, and electronics management systems are generally provided by the automobile assemblers.

NipponDenso assumes complete responsibility for the starter motor development program.[a] It develops appropriate engineering and manufacturing plans to meet Toyota's technical requirements and cost targets. *Continuous improvement in quality and cost is a requirement in this relationship.* Program management and program timing is NipponDenso's responsibility. Appropriate design verification (DV), production and tooling verification (PV), and testing are conducted, and documentation is provided to Toyota to ensure that the starter meets the vehicle-level specifications. Initial samples are also provided so that Toyota's new vehicle can be prototyped and tested at the appropriate time, based on agreed program plans.

The process for developing pricing of the motor is quite interesting. Toyota cost engineers will have established a target price for the starter motor. In large part, this price is determined by establishing a design-to-cost (DTC) objective for the car and from there establishing a DTC objective for manufactured and purchased components, as shown in Figure 2-6. The process of establishing the price is outlined in MIT's recent research, *The Machine That Changed the World:*

> To achieve this target cost, both the assembler and the supplier use *value engineering* techniques to break down the costs of each stage of production, identifying each factor that could lower the cost of each part. Once value engineering is completed, the first-tier supplier designated to design and make each component then enters into mutual bargaining with the assembler, not on the price, but on how to reach the target

---

[a]It is noted that two other approaches to component design are employed: (1) the auto maker develops and designs the parts and the parts makers are given the plans and made responsible for their manufacture, and (2) the auto makers and parts makers jointly develop new auto parts without specifying a particular car model.[12]

and still allow a reasonable profit for the supplier. This process is the opposite of the mass-production approach to price determination.[13]

In order for this approach to work,

the supplier must share a substantial part of its proprietary information about costs and production techniques. The assembler and the supplier go over every detail of the supplier's production process, looking for ways to cut costs and improve quality. In return, the assembler must respect the supplier's need to make a reasonable profit. Agreements between the assembler and supplier on sharing profits give suppliers the incentive to improve the production process, because it guarantees that the supplier keeps all the profits derived from its own cost-saving innovations and *kaizen* activities.[14]

A second feature of lean supply is continually declining prices over the life of a model. . . . the price for the first year's production is a reasonable estimate of the supplier's actual cost plus profit. The assemblers are also well aware of the learning curve that exists for producing practically any item. So they realize that costs should fall in subsequent years, even though raw-materials, costs and wages increase somewhat. Improvements in lean production companies should, in fact, come much faster—that is, learning curves should be much steeper—than in mass-production companies because of *kaizen*, the continuous incremental improvement in the production process.

The question is, who realizes the savings? Again, through mutual discussion and bargaining, the assembler and supplier agree on a cost-reduction curve over the four-year life of the product, with the proviso that any supplier-derived cost savings beyond those agreed upon will go to the supplier. This is the principal mechanism in the lean-supply system for encouraging suppliers to engage in rapid and continuous improvement.[15]

Once production begins, Toyota provides NipponDenso with a rolling production forecast. Near-term production schedules are fixed. NipponDenso produces the required starter motors and delivers starters to Toyota in two wire bins (about two hours' worth) at a time. The starters are delivered in special NipponDenso trucks, which are driven to the Toyota plant and offloaded (by the supplier) at a special location reserved for the delivery of starter motors. This special location is where starters are assembled in the vehicle. The driver unloads two full bins, loads two empty bins, and sweeps/ cleans this area of the Toyota factory. He then takes the appropriate starter motor kanban tickets and returns to the Nippon-Denso factory. The kanban tickets are used to authorize manufacturing of additional starter motors based on Toyota's vehicle-line volume.

It is important to note that purchase orders, receivers, quality documents, and/or invoices have not been mentioned. Such paper work, so burdensome in American industry, does not exist in this system. NipponDenso is paid once per month. Payment is made without an invoice, by multiplying the pre-agreed price per starter by the number of vehicles incorporating this starter produced by Toyota during the month.

Quality and part count problems drive immediate crises. The Toyota factory is immediately shut down if any Toyota employee identifies a quality problem with any component or process. Because there is no idle inventory, Toyota and all its suppliers are affected at once. The supplier or operation involved receives considerable attention. Every resource, both within Toyota and within the now idle supply base, is made available, as necessary, to correct the root problem. Toyota and the supplier trace every defective part to its ultimate cause and take necessary action to ensure that the problem is solved and never recurs. The idle Toyota facility affects every organization in the same way. Mutual enlightened self-interest drives cooperation among these otherwise diverse groups. Problems within the keiretsu are solved quickly.

From the Supplier's Point of View

This section is from an article by David Russell in *Business Tokyo's* April 1990 issue.[b] The article is based on an interview with the Japanese head of a group of several dozen small- and medium-size manufacturing companies who "spoke only on condition of anonymity, fearing," he said, "for the safety of his firms. If I were to speak publicly, especially to a magazine for North American executives, my companies would suffer. The big manufacturers we serve would retaliate by destroying what I have worked all my life to build up!"[16]

> The companies in a manufacturing group are like parts of a big machine. As a subcontractor, you exist to produce goods for the company one level above you. You produce what they want, when they want it, and at the price they want it. Rule No. 1 is never to talk to companies outside the group. From now on, everything you know, everything you see, everyone you meet is in the group. If you go to work for a subsidiary of the Hitachi group, your people have to belong to the Hitachi unions. Why? So that your employees won't accidentally share ideas or information with union members of another group.
>
> As a member of a manufacturer's corporate group, you are automatically a member of its keiretsu industrial group. What this means for you, the small operator, is that you have to do business not only with the companies in your parent's pyramid, but with other firms in its keiretsu.
>
> Just as an example, let's take the Sumitomo Group. Suppose you are a low-ranking supplier to a small subsidiary of NEC. [NEC used to be called Sumitomo Communications Industrial. It is still a core company in the group.] Let's say you want to build a new plant. First you have to borrow funds from Sumitomo Bank. Then you hire a Sumitomo-approved contractor, who purchases his steel, cement, wire, cable, and

---

[b]Reprinted courtesy of *Business Tokyo*, 104 Fifth Avenue, New York, N.Y.

so on from Sumitomo-approved suppliers. You need fire insurance? Sumitomo Marine and Fire is there. Life insurance? Sumitomo Life. I could go on, but you get the idea. Whatever you need, the group supplies it. If not through one of its main group companies, then through a related company. You never use a total outsider. And should you ever be so foolish as to take your account away from a group firm, an executive from the main bank will be on the phone the next day to persuade you to reconsider.

I love it when American politicians start jabbering about opening up "free markets" in Japan—because if you think any of these keiretsu are about to change their ways, you're in for a big surprise.

I know what it's like to run a small business. I started a little company 30 years ago, and my staff and I worked night and day just to stay alive. Over the years that company grew and I started others. Now I've got my own little "group," and I'm proud of the work we do. Some of my firms are so good that they could produce first-rate goods under their own brand name. But none of them ever will.

Why? Because I'm a subcontractor—first, last, and always. My business is to supply high-quality goods to the big companies that know how to market them. I profit because my clients recognize quality. But if I put on the market just one pocket calculator with my own name on it, I become a competitor. Even if I continued to be a subcontractor, people would think my best work went into my own products. I don't want that. As long as I stay out of sight, I'll stay in business.

The problem is that even if you want to go independent, the big companies make it almost impossible. They're afraid that you'll get ideas about going solo, listing your stock, putting your name on their merchandise. Big companies try to discourage this type of thinking by squeezing your profit margins. This keeps their costs down and ensures that your company never becomes strong enough to escape. Don't forget, the parent company controls your income and knows if you're even starting to turn a profit. How? Through your bank, of course.

Once you're part of an industrial group, you have no secrets. Your bank is the group's bank, and your company's financial details are available on request to senior group members. If the parent thinks you're worth anything at all, he'll get you when your company's young and growing and make you one of his permanent suppliers.

This is how they do it: The parent gives you a nice fat order. You fill it. He gives you another, bigger order. You fill most of it. A guy from the main bank comes around and says, "You know, if you added an extra wing on the factory, you could handle a lot more work. For a solid, young firm like yours, I'm sure we could arrange a loan at practically no interest."

While you're considering the idea, the parent offers you another order. "Can you handle it or not?" they ask. "If you can't, just say so and we'll use somebody else." That's it. Once he passes you by, it's over. You may never see a decent order again. They're offering you more work, bigger paychecks, and a chance to expand your operation. What can you do? You take it.

A year or two later they pull the same routine, but this time the parent socks you with a really big order. You tell them you want the order, but it will take time. You don't have the facilities or the staff. "Why not ask the bank for another loan?" the parent says. No, you don't want another loan. "Well, since your firm is doing such good work, why don't we just give you the money?" What's the angle? Simple. Just to help you out, the parent will invest in your firm. Then a couple of the top subsidiary firms will do the same. You can take the money and grow, or turn it down and start laying off staff. Pretty soon you've got orders coming in nice and steady, but a third of your company is owned by your clients. They tell you to put one of their people on your board, so you put him on the board. They tell you to hire a dozen of their guys with a combined IQ of 17 (the parent doesn't want them around), so you hire them. You know one of these guys is just a spy for the parent. But what can you do?

When they tell you to cut prices, you damn well better

find a way to cut them. That's what really hurts. For instance, you get an order from the parent and start up production. A few weeks later one of the parent's managers comes to inspect your plant. He says you've got to lower costs 10 percent. What he means is that the parent wants to lower their costs, so you've got to lower your prices. Of course, the price was fixed when you got the order, but that means nothing. If you want to meet your payroll, you need to keep the orders coming. So you eat the 10 percent—and your profit margin.

A few weeks later he comes back. "Another 5 percent," he says. You rack your brain thinking of ways to speed up production. You put people on all-night shifts, you lower salaries, you do whatever you have to, but you squeeze that extra 5 percent.

Then he comes back again. Maybe he takes out a stopwatch to measure how much you've increased production. "Good job," he says, "but not good enough. We need another 5 percent." You tell him you're up against the wall. He reminds you that there are a lot of other companies just as good as yours that would love to have the contract, but his threats don't matter, because there isn't any room left to increase production or cut costs. That's it.

He thinks awhile. "Okay, I can see you're pretty tight. Maybe we shouldn't push too hard. But this factory would run more smoothly if you got some new machinery." Like what? "Like this," he says, pulling out a catalog. He wants you to buy some new piece of machinery, probably from a keiretsu company, to increase production. You tell him you can't afford it. "Take out a loan," he says. "I'll call the bank and make sure your credit is good." And he's gone. He knows you're in a bind. You can complain, but you'll buy the equipment.

Until recently the subcontractors [lower tier members of a keiretsu] were absolute slaves . . . the Japanese subcontractor isn't in love with his parent company. He's tied to it by tradition and the threat of losing his business.[17]

ATTRIBUTES OF THE JAPANESE KEIRETSU

The Japanese keiretsu is a complex subcontracting organizational environment that has produced remarkable economic results. American business executives must not naively accept these concepts, however, as much of this practice raises serious ethical and legal concerns. The attributes of the Japanese keiretsu, which are receiving critical attention in the Western world, are discussed in Figure 2–7.

CONCLUDING REMARKS

This brief overview of the Japanese keiretsu shows how our Japanese competitors have developed a powerful strategic

FIGURE 2–7
Attributes of the Horizontal Japanese Keiretsu

Feature	Perceived Effects
Cross ownership of stock	Enhances communication Facilitates trust Provides patient money Creates appearance of trade restraint Creates appearance of reciprocity
Interlocking boards of directors	Same
Bank led industrial groups	Improves access to capital Provides patient money Raises questions about independence Redefines the role of banks
Cost and profit control	Drives value-chain competitiveness Limits suppliers' management control Limits suppliers' entrepreneurial activity Institutionalizes lower-tier "underclass"
Supplier/buyer cooperation	Drives quality and productivity improvement Drives competitiveness Limits and restricts market access Limits and restricts new sources

weapon in the global marketplace. As noted in Chapter 1, the Japanese keiretsu has two components: a horizontal one and a vertical one. The horizontal keiretsu provides considerable control through equity ownership and efficient access to capital through its banking members. However, these horizontal activities have been sharply criticized by many American business and political leaders and current U.S. antitrust laws preclude their adoption. The vertical aspect of the Japanese keiretsu, however, contains important principles, many of which are in the American business environment. These principles recognize that constructive competition takes place between value chains, and that competition within value chains is often dysfunctional.

The Japanese vertical keiretsu suffers from an inherent weakness—one which is the basis of superiority of its American counterpart: in Japan many first-, second-, third-, and fourth-tier suppliers are captives of their keiretsu masters with limited flexibility. They are told what to do, how to do it, and how much they will be paid. In many cases, lower-tier suppliers are little more than sweat shops with only one customer and deplorable working conditions.

In Chapter 3, we address how American Keiretsu-type (AKT) relationships combine the benefits of the vertical component of the Japanese keiretsu with the best of American entrepreneurship and technology. The result is a key to global competitiveness!

NOTES

1. Shintaro Ishihara (member, Japanese Diet), *The Japan that Can Say No: Why Japan Will Be First among Equals* (New York: Simon & Schuster, 1991), p. 50. Quoted in Thurow, *Head to Head*, p. 30.
2. Lester Thurow, *Head to Head* (New York: Alfred Morrow and Company, 1992) p. 32.

3. David Friedman, "The Nikkei's Big Surprise: A Quest to Oust Foreigners," *Los Angeles Times* (April 26, 1992), p. M1.
4. David Friedman, *The Misunderstood Miracle* (Cornell University Press, 1988), pp. 25, 29.
5. Marie Anchordoguy, "A Brief History of Japan's Keiretsu," *Harvard Business Review* (July–August 1990), p. 59.
6. Charles H. Ferguson, "Computers and the Coming of the U.S. Keiretsu," *Harvard Business Review* (July–August 1990), p. 63.
7. *Ibid.*, p. 64.
8. David Russell, "The Truth about Big Business in Japan," *Business Tokyo* (April 1990), pp. 23–28.
9. "Learning from Japan," *Business Week* (January 27, 1992) p. 54.
10. Boone Pickens, Letter to the Editor, *Business Week* (February 17, 1992), p. 8.
11. For more insight into this issue, see Ford S. Worthy, "Japan's Smart Secret Weapon," *Fortune* (August 12, 1991), p. 73.
12. "The Relationship between Japanese Auto and Auto Parts Makers," Mitsubishi Research Institute (February 6, 1987).
13. James P. Womack, Daniel T. Jones, and Daniel Roos, *The Machine That Changed the World* (New York: Harper Perennial, 1991), p. 148. Reprinted with the permission of Rawson Associates, an imprint of Macmillan Publishing Company. Copyright © 1990 James P. Womack, Daniel T. Jones, Daniel Roos, Donna Sammons Carpenter.
14. *Ibid.*, p. 149.
15. *Ibid.*, pp. 149–150.
16. Russell, "The Truth," p. 23.
17. *Ibid.*, pp. 24–26.

CHAPTER 3

THE AMERICAN KEIRETSU

U.S. and European companies must build large scale corporate families that are strategically cohesive, yet entrepreneurial and flexible.[1]

Charles H. Ferguson

The American Keiretsu combines the best of the Japanese Supply Management concepts with the best of American entrepreneurship, flexibility, market discipline, and technology. The result is a highly efficient and focused supply structure that can be used as a strategic weapon to provide global competitive advantage. "In short, there's a pressing need for U.S. manufacturers to develop something similar to *keiretsu.*"[2]

In this chapter, we look at the variety of possible supplier relationships, the 12-key prerequisites to forming American Keiretsu-type (AKT) relationships, and then describe the process of establishing an AKT working relationship.

AKT alliances pay big dividends, but they require considerable effort. As noted by Lester Thurow in *Head to Head*, to have influence over others requires *"an institution where there are strong voluntary incentives to participate."*[3] In other words, you can make anyone do what they want to do! Accordingly, such alliances tend to be limited to strategic requirements. Each customer/supplier interface must be evaluated based on a strategic (or importance) criterion. Obviously, some relationships, components, or commodities will be judged to be of greater strategic importance than others. This evaluation process is a first critical step in the identification of those suppliers, components, commodities, and services which, at least initially, appear to contain strategic impact or embody important leverage.

This evaluation must be done periodically and requires the participation of a cross-functional Supply Management group. Obviously, only a limited number of the total purchased inputs will be judged by this group to have potential strategic importance. A detailed discussion of these strategic considerations is provided in Chapter 4.

TYPES OF SUPPLY RELATIONSHIPS

Typically, firms find that they have a variety of supplier relationships ranging from little noticed to high-visibility ones. (See Figure 3–1.) Firms find that their purchased inputs do not fall conveniently into two categories, strategic or nonstrategic, but also range from little noticed to high visibility. The task is to evaluate all these relationships and place each within an appropriate context. Quite obviously, Supply Management must select the most appropriate type of relationship on a case-by-case basis. Supplier relationship management activities are significantly different, dependent on the type of relationship selected. The focus of this book is on high value-added relationships.

Before discussing collaborative relationships, it is appro-

FIGURE 3–1
Supply Relationship Value Model

Arm's Length Relationships			Collaborative Relationships		Ownership
Vendors	Traditional Suppliers	Certified Suppliers	Partnership-Type Relationships	American Keiretsu-Type Alliances	Joint Ventures

◁ Lower Value-Added Relationships   Higher Value-Added Relationships ▷

priate to review briefly the other two supplier/customer relationships that are commonly used.

Arm's-Length Relationships

The very name seems to evoke a negative connotation in the evolving environment of supplier/customer cooperation. However, such a conclusion is improper. Every firm has supplier relationships in this category. As a practical matter, every firm will retain a number of these arm's-length relationships for minor requirements. Examples include vending machines, one-time minor expenses, and/or infrequent low-skill services. The issue isn't a choice between the levels of supplier/customer relationships: the issue is matching the importance of the purchase requirement with the appropriate level of relationship. As one advances along this continuum from left to right, the joint expense, time, and dedication required to establish and sustain relationships increase geometrically. Not every purchase requirement is worth the effort required to develop, nurture, and manage the complex relationships indicated on the right side of Figure 3-1.

Ownership Relationships

The option of taking an equity position in a supplier firm or of forming a joint venture company may represent an appropriate strategic choice, under some circumstances. As seen in Chapter 2, equity participation is a control element in the Japanese keiretsu. At the same time, it is the focus of considerable criticism. In the United States, the success record of joint ventures over the past 20 years has been mixed. Joint venture activity in the U.S. has been down considerably in recent years. Many large firms in the United States are restructuring and eliminating prior acquisitions and joint ventures as part of this activity. The research base in this area is limited; however, preliminary data developed by Jeffrey R. Williams, Betty Lynn Paez, and Leonard Sandards, published in their 1988 article "Conglomerates Revisited,"[4] show:

Acquisition/Divestiture in the United States (1975 to 1984)

Strategic Category	Actions	1975–1979	1980–1984
Horizontal	Acquisitions	32	23
	Divestitures	5	14
Vertical	Acquisitions	10	11
	Divestitures	3	11

Based on these data and other empirical evidence developed by Bruce Kogut in his article, "Joint Ventures: Theoretical and Empirical Perspectives," in the same publication,[5] there is a strong indication that acquisition activity is declining and divestiture activity is increasing in response to increased business complexity, technological change, and increased global competition. These industry restructurings are currently receiving considerable attention in the business press and, therefore, are not further developed here.

A September 21, 1992, *Fortune* article entitled "Are Strategic Alliances Working?" states: "The rate of joint venture formation between U.S. companies and international partners has been growing 27 percent annually since 1985. Are these partnerships achieving the goals set out for them? In many cases the answer is no: Roughly one-third of the 49 alliances tracked by McKinsey were flops, failing to live up to their parents' expectations."[6] Empirical evidence suggests that the rate of success within the United States is similarly disappointing.

ELEMENTS OF AMERICAN KEIRETSU-TYPE RELATIONSHIPS

The focus is on collaborative and, particularly, AKT relationships. Here are the key characteristics of these relationships.

Trust

Based on the extensive research conducted by John Carlisle and Bob Parker, being trustworthy means doing those things that encourage others to trust you. Carlisle and Parker define trust as "Reliably doing what you say you will do."[a]

As discussed later, the potential parties to an AKT relationship start off wanting to trust, but in a cautious mode. As Harmon and Peterson write, "Many suppliers have been reluctant to supply 100 percent of a customer's requirements, even when they have sufficient capacity or would invest in more. They are all too aware of instances where they or other suppliers have had major customers withdraw their business, leaving the company with expensive excess capacity and sometimes forcing it into bankruptcy. In other cases, customers have threatened to go elsewhere to force the supplier to price his products far below a reasonable return on investment."[7]

Potential AKT parties worry about confidentiality. They worry about "what ifs." As several positive reassuring experiences occur, trust grows. While trust cannot be manufactured, it can and should be nurtured. The parties to an AKT relationship must continually examine potential individual actions affecting the relationship for its impact on trust. Osamu Nobuto, president of Mazda Motor Company, in a 1987 address at a senior Ford executive meeting (ironically, on December 7) said, "First is the factor of mutual trust. I

---

[a]The importance of trust is a key to the development and maintenance of AKT relationships. For an in-depth look into this issue, the readers are encouraged to read *Beyond Negotiation: Redeeming Customer-Supplier Relationships* by John A. Carlisle and Robert C. Parker (Chishester, U.K.: John Wiley & Sons, 1989).

believe this cannot be underestimated. Both Mazda and Ford have worked hard to understand each other, to communicate openly, and to respect each other's viewpoints, even when we differ. But, there is obviously more to it than this. Among the factors we see are:

> FIRST: Mutual Benefit. No relationship works when the benefits are not mutually shared.
>
> SECOND: We have also understood and respected each other's independence and the fact that, in the larger scheme of things, we are obviously also competitors."[8]

Long-Term Objectives and Commitments

From initial sourcing on through the evolution of the relationship, the parties to an AKT relationship must share long-term objectives for their areas of interdependency. These shared objectives must result in appropriate commitments in such areas as R&D, capital investment, process improvement, and so forth.

Respect for Others' Rights, Needs, and Opinions

In contrast with its Japanese counterpart, parties to an AKT relationship are equals. They are both enlightened capitalists. While they will experience disagreements and conflicts (just as will occur within a firm between members of functional areas such as engineering, manufacturing, and Purchasing), they must conduct their discussions in an atmosphere of respect and long-term advantage.

Flexibility

AKT relationships are flexible in their time horizon and/or focus. Two firms may decide to cooperate permanently across a selected product and/or process. As an example, a customer may select a single supplier to produce all the customer's screw machine requirements. Contrast this with firms that may decide to focus their cooperation narrowly on a single project. For example, Ford Motor Company's outstanding, and well-publicized, relationship with its competitor Mazda did not preclude it from jointly developing a new mini-van with another competitor, Nissan.

Sensitivity and Empathy for the Other Party

Both partners agree to, and work at, understanding issues that arise from the other party's point of view. This is not to say that they agree with this viewpoint, but they must thoroughly understand it.

Cultural Compatibility

The differences in corporate cultures can be extreme and conflict inevitable. Potential parties to an AKT relationship must examine each other's culture to maximize the probability of a good fit, or at least ensure a thorough understanding of unavoidable differences. The business press is replete with examples of failed business partnerships, joint ventures, and business acquisitions. Many of these failures have been attributed to cultural incompatibility.

Atmosphere of Cooperation

Senior management and the individuals responsible for managing supply contracts and nurturing relationships must establish and maintain an atmosphere of cooperation. (This issue is discussed in greater detail in Chapter 9.)

Acknowledged Interdependence

U.K. authorities David Ford, Richard Lamming, and Richard Thomas observe that "The difficulties in implementing policies such as Partnership and Lean Supply are principally attitudinal, although the attitudes in question reside in several different parts of the business organisation and environment."[9]

All players from both organizations must recognize that "We need them as much as they need us." This attitude must replace the misguided one of "beat the supplier" or "beat the buyer!"

Robert W. Hall, one of the leading manufacturing authorities, states, "Unfortunately, creating new relationships is much more difficult than recognizing the need for them. Learning how to perform differently with suppliers entails changes in technology, business systems, and behavior."[10]

Top Management Support and Active Involvement

As discussed throughout this book, AKT relationships require active top management support. Senior executives from leading firms such as the Tennant Company and General Electric Appliance demonstrate their involvement through semiannual or annual interfaces with their supply partners' senior management. This level of top management involvement is essential if the relationships are to mature— and to survive through both good and bad times!

Shared Risk in Cooperative Projects

Each project must stand alone on its own merits. This project activity dimension provides focus for management and facilitates the measurement of specific project contributions at both firms. Disciplines must be put in place that ensure that these "special" relationships stay focused and do not flow over into product or technical activities (at either firm), which are beyond the scope of agreed cooperation.

Brief Constructive Contracts Focused on Mutual Advantages

We share Dr. W. Edwards Deming's goal of one-page contracts. Obviously, both parties' interests must be protected. One cannot provide for all contingencies; however, both parties can agree to work together in specified areas for mutual gain. Disciplines can be developed that restrict access to areas and/or activities within the scope of cooperation.

Tight Operating Linkages

Communication must be planned for and facilitated through the establishment of tight operating linkages. Intercompany teams and co-location are two examples.

An important emerging requirement identified by the Iacocca Institute of Lehigh University is that "the computers, networks, and software that distributed workers (including suppliers) use must all be mutually compatible. Cooperative work projects can proceed efficiently only if information can flow freely among all of the project members, however widely distributed geographically they may be. . . . Uniform data exchange standards and broadband communication channels are the necessary infrastructure for cooperation to take place."[11]

No Secrets in Areas of Cooperation

Forecasted changes in demand, plans to discontinue a product line, technological advances, supply threats that affect, or may affect, areas of agreed cooperation must all be shared by the parties to an AKT relationship.

Open Books on Common Projects

Forecasts, production plans, and cost data relevant to the project must be shared.

Possible Co-Location Driven by Need and Efficiency

Some companies have learned the advantages of co-location of personnel. Communication, commitment, project control and timing, manufacturability, and quality are all enhanced. However, project-focus and technology-access discipline must be maintained to the extent that the parties to this activity are competitors in other business activities.

In-Depth Knowledge of the Other Party

AKT suppliers are as important to the manufacturer's success and survival as are its customers. Those responsible for the management and nurturing of these relationships must understand the firm's suppliers as well as the firm's marketing department understands its customers.

Frequent Operating Level Contact

As discussed in Chapter 9, operating-level contact must be planned for and managed. Information that *may* be of interest or concern to either party must be made available in a timely manner, not held for the next meeting. The opening rule must be "No Surprises." Supplier engineers, quality professionals, and manufacturing personnel should see firsthand how their products are used by the customer. And customer personnel should see how purchased materials are designed and fabricated.

Managers Responsible for the Relationship

Too often, business relationships are established and then allowed to wither. Successful relationships require active management by both partners. Just as successful marketers appoint account managers, the parties to an AKT relationship must appoint and support supply account managers within

FIGURE 3–2
Typical Elements of American Keiretsu Alliances

Business Elements:
- Long-term common business objectives.
- Vested business interest in others' success.
- Shared risks.
- Open and fast communication.
- Possible co-location.
- Managers of business relationship at both parties.
- Culturally compatible.

Human Relations Elements:
- Mutual trust.
- Mutual respect.
- Top management support and involvement at both parties.
- Open environment.
- Frequent and scheduled contact.

---

both firms. These and other typical elements of AKT relationships are depicted in Figure 3–2.

PREREQUISITES

As shown in Figure 3–3, there are 12 prerequisites to forming successful and viable AKT relationships.

Establish a Strategic Supply Management Initiative with Executive Sponsorship.   Chapter 1 describes the many benefits of strategic Supply Management. In order to gain these benefits, those involved in the Supply Management process must develop an action plan to establish a strategic Supply Management initiative and then secure top management's sponsorship and support. Experience indicates that executive

FIGURE 3–3
Primary Prerequisites to American Keiretsu-Type Relationships

Organizational Commitment Activities
- Establish a strategic supply management initiative with executive sponsorship.
- Obtain top management agreement to play an active role in consummating and nurturing these new relationships.
- Accept the challenge of World Class supply management.
- Develop cross-functional teams.
- Prepare the organization to conduct business in a new way.

Assessment and Evaluation of Current Supply Processes
- Map current processes (qualitatively and quantitatively).
- Benchmark current processes.
- Conduct gap analysis and identify opportunities.

Supply Strategy Development and Implementation
- Apply eight dimensions of supply strategy.
- Integrate supply strategy with corporate and SBU strategies.
- Develop measurement methodology.
- Implement approved strategies.

sponsorship is a critical and necessary element of success. Initiatives that have been undertaken without a senior executive sponsor have a high incidence of failure.

Obtain Top Management Agreement to Play an Active Role in Consummating and Nurturing AKT Relationships. Just as senior management aids the establishment and nurturing of *key* customer accounts, senior managers have *key* roles to play in the establishment and nurturing of *key* AKT relationships.

Accept the Challenge of World Class Supply Management. It is foolhardy to rush into these relationships without first ensuring that the firm's supply system is ready to manage in the new environment. *This is the most common mistake being made by U.S. firms today.*

World Class Supply Management, as briefly described in this book, must be in place. This is no small task and must not be underestimated. (If you and your colleagues rated your Supply Management system as a 3 or less in Chapter 1, you have internal work to do!)

Develop Cross-Functional Supply Teams.[12] The immense opportunities available through the implementation of strategic Supply Management are beginning to receive considerable executive management focus. Gaining the benefits of these opportunities requires a new supply side strategic view, a willing acceptance of change, and a commitment to cross-functional teamwork.

Apart from the sociological reasons for group involvement, there are other critically important reasons requiring the involvement of cross-functional teams. John Carlisle and Bob Parker call cross-functional teams "Mandate Teams."

> The members of a Mandate Team are those to whom everyone in the firm (including the Chairman) would turn to ask, "What are your minimum needs which must be met if your function is to lend its full support to achieving this aim?" People who own and communicate those minimum needs (mandates) can usually be identified by looking at the major areas of activity.[13]

Cultural barriers and individual perspectives blocking change become more pliable as attention turns to bottom-line results. People are more willing to work toward and accept change when they have experienced success and are then able to relate to themselves as contributing change agents.

These cross-functional teams replace vertical hierarchies with horizontal networks. While this transition is both essential and inevitable, it calls for a new style of management and leadership to properly balance the needs of the teams and of the functional areas represented by the team members.[14]

The successful development and implementation of a strategic supply plan demands that cross-functional teams be formally identified and the team members' needs be addressed. These are not wants from a wish list; they are minimum performance specifications, without which total quality, cost, and/or customer service cannot be achieved. Mandate owners, as discussed by Carlisle and Parker, exist throughout the firm and throughout the supplier base. Each mandate owner has specific needs that must be met. The achievement of the considerable opportunities available through strategic Supply Management is ultimately tied to shared benefits within the value chain.

Cross-functional teams are competency led. The teams self-select their leadership based on the project phase to ensure that the most competent team member is able to provide leadership at that point in the project.

The progression from arm's-length (perhaps even adversarial) relations to collaborative ones requires many changes—both within the buyer and the seller organizations and between the two organizations. *The big challenge in the progression to AKT relationships is the development and maintenance of a cooperative cross-functional Supply Management team and a World Class Supply Management process.*

As shown in Figure 3–4, these teams are normally populated with professionals from supply/purchasing, quality, design, process engineering, and operations. Marketing, accounting, and finance may also be involved on a case-by-case basis. Many progressive firms also invite appropriate suppliers and customers to participate. The team must identify strategic sourcing opportunities, develop appropriate procurement strategies, implement sourcing activities, and manage the ongoing relationships. It must speak with one voice outside the firm. Experience indicates that these cross-functional

FIGURE 3–4
The Extended Supply Management System

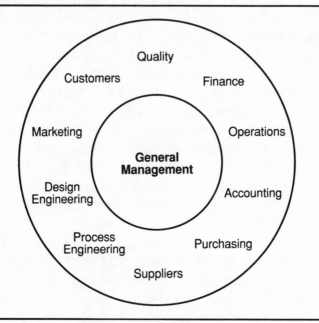

supply teams will require professional team building and training.[b]

Prepare the Organization to Conduct Business a New Way.
Strategic Supply Management requires a new approach to conducting business. Experience has demonstrated that many members of the supply team will not be ready for such a quantum leap. The following and related issues must be addressed:

- Are suppliers sometimes viewed as necessary evils—as the source of problems—as competitors for profits? Such attitudes—at any level—will damage or destroy

---

[b]For insight into the screening and selection of team members, see *Teamwork: What Must Go Right/What Can Go Wrong* by Carl E. Larson and Frank M. J. La Fasto (Newbury Park, Calif.: Sage Publications, 1989).

the most carefully crafted arrangements. Key suppliers are every bit as important as key customers. The firm's customers are its suppliers' customers. Outstanding products and service to the manufacturer's customer is clearly in the mutual interest of the parties to an AKT relationship.

- AKT relationships require both parties to share relevant cost data, sales projections, production schedules, potential problems, capital plans, and so forth. The customer firm must be ready to share as much information as it expects to receive from its supply partners.

- Does the customer possess the discipline required of an outstanding customer? Does it adhere to near-term production schedules? Is it willing to provide adequate lead time for schedule changes? Is it aggressive in the use of just-in-time (JIT), electronic data interchange (EDI), on-line communications, and so forth?

Map Current Processes (Qualitatively and Quantitatively).
The Procurement Processes at the vast majority of firms have evolved through time, based on a reactive approach to Purchasing. Experience suggests that the correlation between management's understanding of these processes and the actual processes is not strong. This situation drives the need to thoroughly evaluate the current processes so that adjustments and efficiencies can be implemented.

Benchmark Current Processes. The process mapping activity identified the processes; now their effectiveness must be determined based on a selected criterion. The benchmarking activity is one method of evaluating this effectiveness and identifying areas of opportunity for improvement and productivity. The subject of benchmarking will be discussed in more detail in Chapter 10.

Conduct Gap Analysis and Identify Opportunities. Quite obviously, this is the bottom line to the previous analysis. Strategic Supply Management implementation offers considerable productivity improvement potential. Efficiencies in reduced bidding, summary invoicing, electronic data interchange (EDI), and other innovations can drive a 30 percent to 70 percent reduction in paperwork and significantly reduce clerical work requirements. Other opportunities involving requirements development, sourcing, negotiation, cost management, technology access, inventory reductions, and other important areas have the potential to contribute significant value to the firm.

Apply the Eight Dimensions of Supply Strategy. Supply strategy is not a monolith. There are eight distinctive considerations, each of which requires serious evaluation. Chapter 4 is dedicated to this topic.

Integrate Supply Strategy with Corporate and SBU Strategies. This is a critically important concept and requirement. Clearly, if the firm is to develop sourcing initiatives that optimize the value contribution potential, then these activities must be appropriately aligned with other strategic objectives of the business to be effective. This requirement is another driver of the logic behind the use of cross-functional teams. Strategic intent and internal compatibility are vital to success.

Develop Measurement Methodology. There are two aspects to measurement: the process of monitoring implementation progress and the identification and quantification of the increased value contribution being achieved through American Keiretsu implementation. Strategic Supply Management concepts offer considerable improvement opportunity. Initiatives are generally self-funding. Savings of 20 to 40 times the cost of implementation are not uncommon. Additional discussion on measurement will be presented in Chapter 9.

Implementation of Approved Strategies. Implementation provides the payoff for these actions. It is discussed in Chapter 10.

FORMING THE UMBRELLA AGREEMENT

The AKT alliance begins with an agreement between the firm and its immediate supplier. Ideally, this will progress up the value chain to include other suppliers. However, each relationship is independent and is based on value contribution as perceived and/or measured by the buyer and seller firms involved. Anton Peisl, a member of the Board of Siemens AG, writes, ''If companies are to pursue competitiveness and form alliances flexibly, they cannot be restricted a priori in their choice of partners.''[15] Obviously, firms are free to engage in sourcing activities as they see fit, based on their analysis of the resultant competitive advantage opportunities. Each party is involved in joint activities including:

- Production and efficiency improvement planning.
- New product development/component design coordination.
- Rationalization of manufacturing, test, and logistics resources.
- Cost management and control efforts.
- Constant process, product, and logistics improvement.

A successful AKT relationship is built on the premise that the basic needs of both members must be satisfied. It maximizes each member's core strength. No matter how well the relationship is structured, it is the people involved that will make it or break it!

In the vast majority of cases, AKT candidates will be present-day suppliers. There will be exceptions, as some present-day suppliers will be judged incapable and others will have little incentive to improve. When these situations are identified, the firm is required to conduct research to find acceptable alternatives. Obviously, the development of an AKT agreement with a new supplier may be more challenging than with an existing one. However, the benefits outlined in Chapter 1, together with the desire of both parties to gain a competitive advantage, should compress the time normally involved in transitioning from supplier to AKT supplier.

The AKT Relationship Life Cycle

Figure 3–5 portrays a typical AKT relationship's life cycle. Prior to entering into preliminary discussions, the buying firm will have determined which component, commodity, services, or equipment offer improvement potential to the firm's survival and success. The buying firm will also have determined that an AKT relationship is essential in meeting the buying firm's needs and those of its supplier for the item or commodity. And it will have monitored the supply environment to identify the most attractive potential AKT supplier.

The process of forming the umbrella agreement between buyer and seller is described in some detail in this section. It should be noted that many specific projects may be undertaken under this umbrella agreement. Each of these projects will have its specific characteristics and life and will tend to parallel the resultant end product's life cycle.

Figure 3–5 indicates that forces may come into play to cause the umbrella agreement to enter a state of decline. This may be a logical result of forces such as changes in technology, changing foci by either or both firms, changes in key personnel, and so on. However, when either party to an AKT relationship becomes aware that decline in the relationship appears to be settling in, a close and careful joint study should be undertaken to determine if the parties should attempt to

FIGURE 3-5
Innovation and Technology Impact on Product Life Cycles

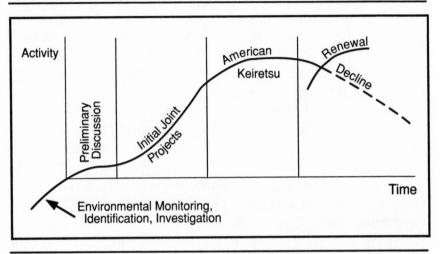

renew and reinvigorate the relationship. If renewal is in the interest of both parties, an outside mediator/facilitator may play a constructive role.

"It is important to understand before initiating an outsourcing relationship, under what general conditions it should be modified or terminated. This calls for an initial and ongoing evaluation of your own intentions, supplier intentions, and the evolution of technology. . . . Over time, supplier intentions should become more clear and dictate a termination, continuance, or extension of the relationship."[16]

Getting Started

Once members of the cross-functional supply team have identified, researched, and thoroughly screened a candidate AKT supplier, a meeting of the respective corporate or division COO's should be established. The objective of this meeting is the creation of an executive oversight committee consisting of the two COO's. The oversight committee appoints appropriate individuals from the two firms to explore the merits and then the details of a formal AKT relationship. Two of these individuals, one from each firm, will be assigned primary relationship responsibility.[c] The details will be contained in a written agreement in the form of a short memorandum of understanding (MOU) to be submitted to the executive committee for approval or disapproval.

The principal reason for reducing the agreement to writing is to encourage a continuation and growth in the relationship that survives personnel changes. More detailed issues addressing specific projects will be negotiated on a case-by-case basis (as described in Chapters 5 through 7). The MOU is simply that—an agreement to work together in a mutually beneficial, synergistic relationship.

Benjamin Franklin is attributed with the following note at the end of a very long letter to his daughter: ''Please excuse the length of this letter. I did not have time to write a shorter one.'' Brief agreements between AKT parties are highly recommended; however, this is not to imply that these agreements will not require considerable time to develop. They should establish ground rules on how to determine prices, quality objectives, proprietary rights, and any other issues of concern to the parties. These written documents must be true manifestations of the higher-level agreements of the parties. This process demands that each party first thoroughly understand specifically why it is interested in an arrangement with this particular candidate and what specific advantages it expects to gain over time.

Step one is for each firm independently to develop a written understanding of the agreement as it views it, taking special care to list the advantages it expects to achieve.

Step two is to exchange these documents. Each firm must study the other firm's vision and attempt to identify ap-

---

[c]Relationship responsibility will be discussed further in Chapter 9.

proaches that would achieve the other firm's goals while meeting its own objectives.

Step three is to meet and develop a memorandum of understanding under which specific projects can be developed and negotiated on a case-by-case basis. It is very important that early agreements address intellectual property rights and rights to future joint innovations since this is an area of special concern and requires a disciplined approach.

Perhaps the most challenging issue to address in these broad level discussions is the principle that both members of the AKT relationship must work to help the other firm become World Class.

The Negotiating Team

The negotiating teams should be small and balanced. The pro forma customer team consists of the senior representatives of product development, operations, engineering, and purchasing. This structure recognizes the essentiality of senior-level involvement and commitment on both sides while involving those managers who will be most responsible for implementing the agreement on a project by project basis. Representatives of quality, marketing, customer support, and finance should be available on an "as required" basis, remembering that the objective is to reach an agreement in principle—not in detail.

Culture

The two largest impediments to the development of successful AKT relationships are trust and culture. Trust requires time and a number of rewarding experiences to develop.

On the other hand, cultural differences must be addressed before the two teams commence discussions. Each team should work to understand the other's culture—what is important to them and how they see things. Normally, insight into another organization's culture is available with minimal effort.

If the customer firm is dealing with representatives of a foreign-based firm, the American team must possess or develop a minimum understanding of the culture and the language.

Time

Rapport should be developed before rushing into business discussions. Social evenings and visits to each other's operating locations lay the foundation for fruitful discussions. This foundation-building will take much longer with a foreign supplier since it will insist on knowing the potential customer's experience, motives, expertise, methods of communication, ethics, and plans in great detail before moving on to the heart of the discussions. By the way, much can be said for this cautious approach to developing relationships!

Confidentiality

Neither party should disclose any information (technical, financial, market, etc.) that it considers to be proprietary or confidential until both parties have entered into a mutual confidentiality disclosure agreement. Such an agreement will create an ethical and trusting environment.

Normally, proprietary disclosures will go through a sequence of steps. Generally, discussions will begin by addressing business concepts and areas of mutual interest. More sensitive information is shared as mutual interest, a need to know, and the likelihood of forming an AKT alliance increase.

The Need for Openness

Each party's real needs must be explored in detail. Forecasts and long-term plans, expectations in the areas of quality, flexible manufacturing, likely new technology thrusts, R&D, and plant and equipment investment needs and plans are all candidates for discussion as an atmosphere of respect and trust develops. And once again for emphasis: each supplier's willingness to work with its key suppliers to bring them to World Class status must be addressed and agreed upon.

DOCUMENTING AND PUBLICIZING RESULTS

The documentation and publicizing of results flowing from the implementation of strategic Supply Management and the resulting AKT relationships is essential *if the effort is to receive essential continuing management support*. Our colleague, Bob Paul, former vice president Materiel at Lockheed, placed great emphasis on publicizing Supply Management's contributions to Lockheed's financial success. In addition to reporting dollar savings, Bob Paul translated the savings to earnings per share and also to the number of dollars of additional sales required to obtain an equivalent impact on the bottom line.

Very careful attention must be paid to reporting credibility. Reported improvements must be real and the methods used to calculate reported improvements must be published and understood. An example of the kind of difficulties involved was observed in one large firm's Purchasing department. Purchasing had been reporting impressive savings for years. Senior management wasn't so impressed when it was discovered that Purchasing identified savings by subtracting the low bid price from the average bid price. It then reported this difference as a savings.

The reporting classifications system shown in Figure 3–6 is introduced as an example. Those outside of the Supply Management system should be encouraged to review documented savings to satisfy themselves as to the validity of the claimed savings.

Many of the benefits resulting from the implementation

of the principles and practices set forward in this book will be very real, but difficult to quantify. The bottom-line implications of reductions in the time-to-market, access to new technologies, and reductions in incoming defects may require "guesstimation." Ideally, members of the cross-functional Supply Management team (ensuring that marketing is represented) should pool their knowledge and wisdom. Their collective estimate should be reviewed and approved at the vice president or director level prior to dissemination.

CONCLUDING REMARKS

AKT relationships are based on trust; shared long-term objectives and commitments; respect for the other's rights, needs, and opinions; sensitivity and empathy for the other party; cultural compatibility; cooperation; interdependence; and top management support and active involvement. Risk is shared in cooperative projects. Brief agreements focusing on mutual advantages are the norm. Tight operating linkages are established. There are no secrets in the areas of cooperation. There is frequent operating level contact. And, of great importance, each party appoints and supports supply account managers whose responsibilities include project management and control, ensuring mutual understanding of both parties' needs and capabilities, communication, and related tasks.

Having established an understanding of AKT relationships, we now turn our attention to the remaining strategic keys to successful Supply Management: "The Eight Dimensions of a Supply Strategy."

FIGURE 3–6
Cost Reduction Measurement Concept

One-Time Savings:

Projected | Savings have been identified and are under contract. Contract performance is either incomplete or not initiated at this time. The total amount of savings will be realized in the current year. One-time savings opportunities will not continue year to year.

Realized | Savings have been identified, are under contract, and contract performance has been initiated. These savings represent the completed portion of that performance. One-time savings opportunities will not continue year to year. Realized savings are a subset of projected savings.

Annualized Savings:

Projected | Savings have been identified and are under contract. Contract performance is either incomplete or not initiated at this time. The total amount of savings will be realized in the current year. These savings will reduce the total cost base and continue year to year.

Realized | Savings have been identified, are under contract, and contract performance has been initiated. These savings represent the completed portion of that performance. These savings reduce the total cost base and continue year to year. Realized savings are a subset of projected savings.

Cost Avoidances: | These savings do not reduce an established cost base. They are the result of cost reduction efforts that take place prior to the establishment of a cost base. They are included as a memo only and are not included in any performance measures. Examples would include fractional head count, process time savings, a negotiation that further reduces the price offered by the lowest bidder prior to an award, the extension of time prior to the implementation of an approved cost increase.

NOTES

1. Charles H. Ferguson, "Computers and the Coming of the U.S. Keiretsu," *Harvard Business Review* (July–August, 1990), p. 56.
2. "Learning from Japan."
3. Lester Thurow, *Head to Head* (New York: Alfred Morrow and Company, 1992), p. 120.
4. Jeffrey R. Williams, Betty Lynn Paez, and Leonard Sandards, "Conglomerates Revisited," *Strategic Management Journal* 9 (1988), pp. 411.
5. Bruce Kogut, "Joint Ventures: Theoretical and Empirical Perspectives," *Strategic Management Journal* 9 (1988), pp. 319–32.
6. Stratford Sherman, "Are Strategic Alliances Working?" *Fortune* (September 21, 1992), p. 77.
7. Roy L. Harmon and Leroy D. Peterson, "Reinventing the Factory," *Productivity Breakthroughs in Manufacturing Today* (New York: Free Press, 1990), p. 258.
8. Osamu Nobuto, Remarks to Ford Motor Company (December 7, 1987), printed.
9. David Ford, Richard Lamming, and Richard Thomas, "Relationship Strategy, Development, and Purchasing Practice," *Proceedings of the 8th IMP Conference,* Lyon, France (September 3–5, 1992), p. 141.
10. Robert W. Hall, "Forward to *Co-Makership: The New Supply Strategy for Manufacturers* by Giorgio Merli (Cambridge, MA: Productivity Press, 1991), p. xiii.
11. *21st Century Manufacturing Enterprise Strategy* (Bethlehem, PA: Iacocca Institute, Lehigh University, 1991), pp. 41, 44.
12. This material is based on Michael F. Doyle's article, "Cross-Functional Implementation Teams," *Purchasing World* (1991).
13. Personal interview with Mr. Parker (November 1991).
14. Larry Hirschhorn and Thomas Gilmore, "The New Boundaries of the 'Boundaryless' Company," *Harvard Business Review* (May–June 1992), p. 104.
15. Anton Peisl, Letter to the Editor, "Can a Keiretsu Work in America?" *Harvard Business Review* (September–October 1990), p. 180.
16. Richard A. Bettis, Stephen P. Bradley, and Gary Hamel, "Outsourcing and Industrial Decline," *Academy of Management Executive* 6, no. 1 (1992), p. 20.

CHAPTER 4

EIGHT DIMENSIONS OF A
SUPPLY STRATEGY

Boundaries will become so fluid that corporations will become temporary arrangements among entrepreneurial cadres. Except for high volume, capital intensive work, every big company will be a confederation of small ones. All small organizations will be constantly in the process of linking up into big ones.[1]

Robert Reich

A thorough, well thought-out supply strategy is at the heart of any successful strategic supply effort. Upstream American Keiretsu-type (AKT) relationships are ones initiated by the buying firm, based on its supply strategy. (The initiation of AKT relationships by sellers was addressed in Chapter 1.) The preparation and development of a supply strategy require input and participation from representatives of the entire Supply Management system. The strategy is *not* Purchasing's plan. Many firms assign their planning staff or business planning organization to manage the development of their supply strategies. At other firms, Purchasing heads this effort. But, in any event, Purchasing is only one of several active participants.

SUPPLY STRATEGY[2]

The supply strategy is the firm's plan for the optimization of its purchased inputs. At most companies, these inputs represent between 20 percent and 70 percent of the firm's net sales. And, as the Japanese keiretsu has shown over the years, leveraging these expenditures can have considerable direct impact on the firm's quality, market share, and competitiveness. One senior Japanese auto executive was recently overheard saying: ''If all you get for your purchase dollar is parts—you lose.'' *This supply strategy must be integrated with the goals, objectives, and strategies of the firm.*

Figure 4–1 is an adaptation of a traditional strategic planning model that has been modified to address the Supply Management planning process. It is included to demonstrate that the strategic Supply Management planning process shares an identical theoretical core with other, more familiar, strategic planning processes.

Available literature on procurement and Supply Management strategy is limited, although there has been an increase, both in volume and quality, in the past few years. Even with this recent activity, the literature base is small relative to the outstanding work available in the area of marketing strategy and corporate strategy in general. One result of this limited research base is that Supply Management strategy is poorly defined, even within the few professional Purchasing/procurement/materiel/supply organizations. Additionally, Supply Management strategy is generally viewed as a monolith. *Nothing could be further from the truth.*

Figure 4–2, ''Strategic Supply Management Complexity,'' integrates the five required improvement goals of quality, technology, velocity, risk reduction, and total cost with the Procurement Process (which will be discussed in later chapters). Additionally, this model identifies the eight dimensions of Supply Management strategy. The complexity involved in the development of a successful supply plan as represented in this model has been seriously underestimated and misunderstood by both academics and practitioners.

This misunderstanding is directly responsible for much of the difficulty American firms have had in attempting to

FIGURE 4–1
Traditional Strategic Planning Model

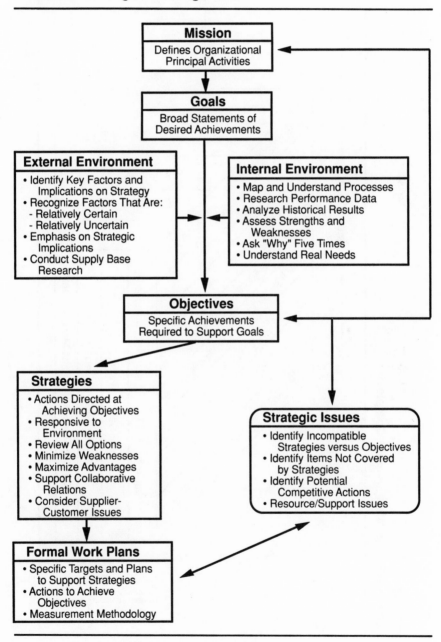

FIGURE 4–2
Strategic Supply Management Complexity

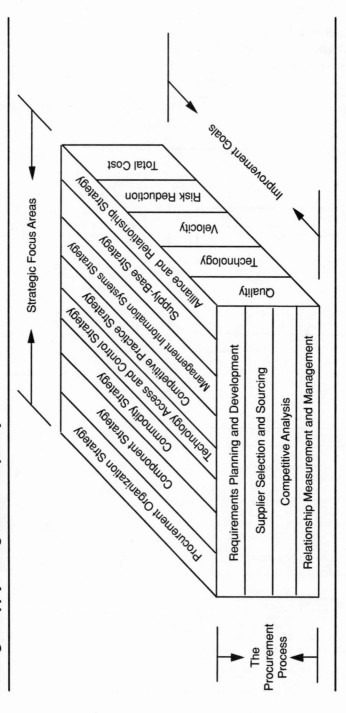

develop Supply Management improvement programs. Many of these suboptimal programs have names like "the supplier alliance program," "the partnership relationships program," "the fewer suppliers program," "the supplier TQP program," and so forth. This is not to say that the basis for these programs is unsound; quite the contrary, the basis for these programs is outstanding. It's the internal planning, organizational understanding, complexity, and commitment that have been inadequate. Like most business decisions, there are multiple facets to all sourcing decisions. For example, technology can flow the wrong way without careful source selection and management attention. Firms wishing to take advantage of the leverage opportunities, efficiencies, and competitive advantages available through strategic Supply Management must formally address each of these eight strategic dimensions.

Purchasing Organization Strategy

There are two unique issues that require formal attention in the area of organization strategy. First, the firm must decide how to organize the Purchasing or materials management department to maximize its contribution. Such action is based on the specifics of the firm's culture, markets, supply environment, challenges, and opportunities. Second, the firm must decide how to organize the Supply Management function to optimize the efficiency of the Procurement Process. *The Supply Management function or process involves many, frequently all, departments within the firm.*

Organizing the Procurement Function
At the department level, many firms see the organizational choices as boiling down to the age-old debate over centralization versus decentralization. This view is too simplistic. As shown in Figure 4–3, "The Centralization/Decentralization Continuum," the organizational choice for most firms must

involve a thorough evaluation of all the options that lie between these two extreme positions.

Some firms may find that a choice to centralize or to
decentralize optimizes the ability of their Purchasing department to contribute. However, the vast majority of companies
will end up with a hybrid organization positioned between
these two extremes. Based on its specific needs, this hybrid
organization must be customized by each company. This organizational choice must offer a reasonable trade-off by maximizing perceived organizational strengths with perceived
organizational weaknesses. Figure 4–3 outlines, at a conceptual level, the types of choices and considerations available.

Organizing the Procurement Process
Tying Supply Management organizational considerations directly to Purchasing organizational considerations is considerably more complex than one might anticipate. A convenient
way to think about this concept is by using a familiar communications model (Sender → Mode → Receiver). This simple
model consists of a sender, a receiver, and a mode. The
sender in this model represents anyone in the organization
with a need for a purchased input. These people are often
called requisitioners. The mode represents the Procurement
Process and the receiver represents the supplier.

The vast majority of American firms currently operate
their Procurement Process as depicted in the above model.
Paper requisitions are sent over the transom to Purchasing.
The buyer often has a limited technical background and little
direct understanding of the requisitioner's real needs. The
buyer transmits the needs (as best possible), as written or
otherwise described by a very busy requisitioner, to three or
more suppliers as effectively as possible. The suppliers (twice
removed from the requisitioner's real need) develop bids or
quotes to satisfy their understanding of the need and send
their written proposals to the buyer. The buyer evaluates
these bids, negotiates commercial terms, selects the winning

FIGURE 4–3
Centralization vs. Decentralization Continuum

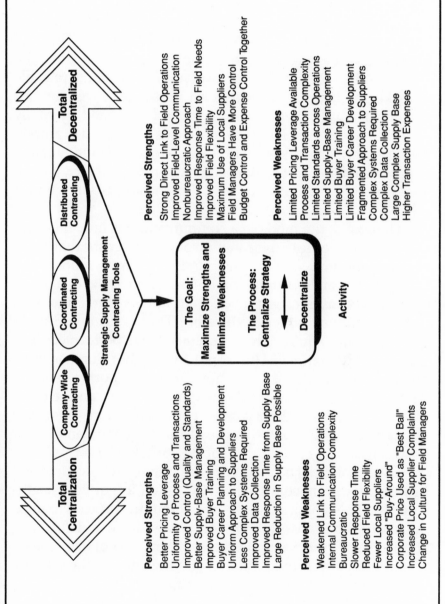

Total Centralization

Company-Wide Contracting

Coordinated Contracting

Distributed Contracting

Total Decentralized

Strategic Supply Management
Contracting Tools

The Goal:
Maximize Strengths and
Minimize Weaknesses

The Process:
Centralize Strategy

Decentralize

Activity

Perceived Strengths

Better Pricing Leverage
Uniformity of Process and Transactions
Improved Control (Quality and Standards)
Better Supply-Base Management
Improved Buyer Training
Buyer Career Planning and Development
Uniform Approach to Suppliers
Less Complex Systems Required
Improved Data Collection
Improved Response Time from Supply Base
Large Reduction in Supply Base Possible

Perceived Weaknesses

Weakened Link to Field Operations
Internal Communication Complexity
Bureaucratic
Slower Response Time
Reduced Field Flexibility
Fewer Local Suppliers
Increased "Buy-Around"
Corporate Price Used as "Best Ball"
Increased Local Supplier Complaints
Change in Culture for Field Managers

Perceived Strengths

Strong Direct Link to Field Operations
Improved Field-Level Communication
Nonbureaucratic Approach
Improved Response Time to Field Needs
Improved Field Flexibility
Maximum Use of Local Suppliers
Field Managers Have More Control
Budget Control and Expense Control Together

Perceived Weaknesses

Limited Pricing Leverage Available
Process and Transaction Complexity
Limited Standards across Operations
Limited Supply-Base Management
Limited Buyer Training
Limited Buyer Career Development
Fragmented Approach to Suppliers
Complex Systems Required
Complex Data Collection
Large Complex Supply Base
Higher Transaction Expenses

Source: Developed in cooperation with Mr. John Armstrong, American President Lines, Ltd.

supplier, and issues a purchase order (P.O.). The supplier's engineers develop and/or manufacture the required materials, ship the materials, and invoice the customer. The buying firm receives the materials, checks the materials for quality, and moves the materials to the appropriate location. The buying firm receives the supplier's invoice, checks it against the P.O. and the receiving report, and notifies accounts payable to make payment. This process is the source of well over 50 percent of all the paper generated and managed by many American firms (see Figure 2-5). In this simplified example, it is apparent that the Procurement Process includes many departments, not just Purchasing. As a matter of fact, if measured based on relative activity, Purchasing plays a minor role.

The role of the mode in a communications model is critical. Communications research strongly suggests that communication improves as the mode becomes more user-friendly. As an example, radio has been judged a more effective communication mode than newspapers, and T.V. has been judged superior to radio. Thus, effective Supply Management requires that Purchasing be performed in a user-friendly manner. This is not to say that Purchasing is not important: the issue is, how is this important service delivered by *Purchasing* to its customers? How can the organization best ensure successful communication; minimize elapsed time; eliminate overhead; and, at the same time, ensure financial control and sound commercial terms?

Given this brief background, organizing the Procurement Process may seem complex; but in reality, it is quite straightforward. The Japanese have engineered this process to maximize efficiency. Most U.S. companies have not formally studied their Procurement Process. Many do not even recognize the organizational difference between Purchasing (the department) and the Procurement Process.

Process understanding is an essential first step in any effectiveness assessment. Firms interested in evaluating the potential benefits outlined in this book as they may apply specifically to their environment, industry, and competitive situation will first have to map their current Procurement Process. A thorough understanding of the entire process flow from product design to project termination is required.

As an example, this process flow should include (but not be limited to) processes involved in:

- Requirements identification.
- Component design—specification development.
- Source identification.
- Competitive practices.
- Source selection.
- Negotiations and contracting.
- Order history.
- Price patterns and history.
- Invoicing, invoice processing, and payment.
- Inbound freight patterns.

Any Procurement Process redesign will require in-depth analysis and a thorough understanding of the current process. As so many firms have learned when attempting to implement total quality management, improvement cannot be maintained without changing the process that drives suboptimal results in the first place. (This subject is addressed in greater detail in Chapter 10.)

COMPONENT STRATEGY

The basis for a sound component strategy is a thorough analysis of the materials required by, and used in, the firm's operations. This analysis can be completed relatively quickly and inexpensively. The process requires knowledgeable individuals from engineering, quality, manufacturing, Purchasing, and possibly others to review the firm's manufactured and purchased components and to classify each. The classifications may vary by firm but typically should include (but not be limited to) the following:

Part cost	Current technology
Technology leverage and trends	Quality leverage
Manufacturing capacity	Criticality to the product
Supply availability	Leverage on the product

This classification system must be designed to allow the team to identify those components that have potential, current, or future strategic importance. This unique importance may involve technology, cost, or even marketing. An obvious example would be the Intel i486™ microprocessor's strategic importance to those personal computer manufacturers that have selected this architecture and use this component in their products, and even in their advertising.

Less Obvious Candidates

A firm's strategic components may not all be as obvious as this microprocessor example. However, experienced working-level managers should be able to identify most such components with relative ease. Often, strategic component candidates are not the current high-visibility items. Therefore, they may be a little more difficult to identify. Strategic components have a significant impact on the business that warrants this special attention.

Strategic Component Dynamics

This relationship will change over time as competition and technology reposition the business and its products. Therefore, the component strategy must be maintained and updated as part of the firm's ongoing strategic planning process. The change in strategic importance over time can be simply illustrated using automobiles and engines. Not long ago, auto engines would clearly qualify as being uniquely strategic components. They were internally designed and produced for the exclusive use of a particular auto firm. The general public held strong views regarding brand images that included the engine. This thinking was encouraged by brand advertising. Based on these market conditions, automobile manufacturers did not purchase engines from outside suppliers; even trading engines between car divisions of the same firm was avoided for a long time.

Contrast this with today: most auto manufacturers proudly announce that selected automobiles carrying their brand name and offered for sale through their dealer network are partially or totally produced for them by other firms. The concept of sourcing the entire automobile is now common. For example, the Pontiac Le Mans is produced by Daewoo, the Ford Fiesta is produced by Kia, and the Dodge Colt is produced by Mitsubishi. Based on this market development, engines may no longer be considered uniquely strategic. Market opinion has shifted; so has technology. The microprocessor that drives the engine control computer may well have replaced the engine as *the* uniquely strategic component.

Another example involves a Fortune 500 firm in the paper industry. This firm realized, as part of its procurement strategy development, that a waste product it purchased from the spot scrap market would soon become a top strategic purchased item. The firm was able to focus management attention, realign organizational responsibilities, and give full-time attention to the purchase of high-quality secondary fiber. The firm established a unique logistics network in a way that will provide competitive marketing advantage in forthcoming years.

Strategic Component Plans

Once a firm's strategic components have been identified, a formalized supply plan must be developed and approved for each. The basic question that the supply plan must answer is: *How can our firm gain continuing access to this critical input component (or service) in an optimum, long-term, advantageous way?* A cross-functional team should be assigned to develop a supply plan that addresses each identified strategic component. The team members must consider appropriate possible alternatives. The approved plan is assigned to the appropriate functional organization for implementation; however, the entire cross-functional supply team remains responsible for results. This process ensures that the same functional groups responsible for the success of the product also play an active role in the procurement decisions for strategic components.

COMMODITY STRATEGY

The commodity strategy is quite similar to the component strategy and equally important. There is considerable confusion regarding the terms "commodity" and "commodity class." Commodities are groups of similar components. One can think of a commodity as a shopping basket of similar items that are purchased together from one source in order to maximize value, efficiency, leverage, and so forth, for both the buyer and the seller. Some firms have developed parts groupings called commodity classes. These groupings may or may not be appropriate as they may or may not represent technology or market structure. *The goal is to group commodities as closely as possible to the market.* Using the earlier example, if the microprocessor were judged to be a strategic component, the balance of the required semiconductors (transistors, resistors, capacitors, etc.) could represent a commodity or two or more commodities.

There are two critical steps in the commodity sourcing strategy process. The first step is the identification of appropriate commodity classifications. The question of what to include, or not include, in a commodity is the issue. Using the example of semiconductors, would an optimum commodity strategy include all semiconductors, or could important advantages be gained by grouping active components as one group and passive components as another? Still another approach would group transistors as one commodity, resistors as another, and so on. The rule of thumb in the development of a commodity grouping is to keep the commodity as large (all-inclusive) as possible. Natural boundaries will limit the size of the commodity. These boundaries include major differences in technology, supply base, logistics, and channels. During the second step, the cross-functional supply team develops an optimum sourcing strategy, similar to the strategy development process used for strategic components.

TECHNOLOGY ACCESS AND CONTROL STRATEGY

Technology Access

Chapter 1 discussed technology access as one of the five basic goals of the American Keiretsu. This section outlines some of the ways this goal is realized. The component and commodity strategy development process offers a rich opportunity for both the consideration and acquisition of current and future technology. This presupposes that the firm has developed a formalized technology road map or a listing of critical present and future technologies, and that this information is available for inclusion in sourcing strategy deliberations.

All suppliers own important design and process technology. Often, technology that is discounted as standard practice at one level in a value chain offers important opportunities at another level of the same value chain. This observation is the basis of the first technology access opportunity. As strategic sourcing selections are made by knowledgeable individuals, technology opportunities can be identified and included in the negotiation process. And, since these strategic selections are typically made with a view toward the development of a jointly profitable long-term relationship, the framework and the atmosphere are much more conducive to achieving success.

The second technology access opportunity involves supplier R&D spending. The motivation for any firm to fund R&D efforts and develop technology is clear. Unfortunately, the connection between R&D funding, product innovation, revenue growth, and profits is not clear. This less than obvious relationship exists in the face of considerable evidence demonstrating that the technology developer is often not the firm that enjoys the fruits of its innovation. In addition to problems converting new technologies into successful products, many manufacturers suboptimize their profit potential from available technology: *there is a breakdown or weakness within their upstream supply chain that blocks the utilization of technology that is developed within the chain.*

A few innovative firms have jointly directed R&D programs tied to the level of sourcing revenue. These agreements offer outstanding opportunities to leverage research engineering resources. Agreements typically establish a pool of funds for directed R&D research. The level of funding is determined by the buyer and the seller as a percent of annual sourcing revenues. As an example, track an important supplier with a history of funding R&D at a rate equal to 5 percent of its revenues. A major customer's sourcing strategy team has selected this supplier as the best possible source for an important purchase requirement. This sourcing decision will drive $5 million in revenue per year with the supplier. Given the supplier's R&D funding history, one could reasonably expect 5 percent or $250,000 to be added to the supplier firm's R&D budget per year. These two companies could agree to cooperate and direct some portion of this incremental R&D funding to the specific future technology needs of the customer. The "hits" on R&D funds so directed would produce a guaranteed market for future sales by the supplier. This is part of the magic in the American Keiretsu concept. *The buying firm purchases required components competitively and receives some "directed" R&D effort as a bonus. The seller supplies this important customer with production materials and gains the opportunity to make a significant contribution to its own future business through customer-directed R&D efforts. Both sides win!*

Technology Control

Obviously, the flow of technology can be a two-way street. Technology transfer involving American industry has had a mixed record over the past 20 years. Many firms have entered supplier relationships with the best of intentions, only to find later that they have actually helped fund a new and very powerful competitor. This "funding" often takes place at two levels: first, through cash flow from the firm's component sourcing actions; and second, through the unintended outflow of proprietary technology, processes, market knowledge, and channels information.

It is impossible to overemphasize the strategic implications surrounding technology control. As early as 1981, Edward Lesnick, Assistant to the President of Wang Laboratories, stated that the computer industry "must police itself to reduce the flow of technology across the Pacific which then, through massive Japanese government support, can turn around and threaten the very companies that provided the technology. It is not a case of the normal competitive activities on which our and most of the world's economic system is based," he said. "But it is a case of the Japanese government directing, financing and, in partnership with Japanese industry, taking all possible steps in order to assure market-share dominance if not outright control."[3] On the one hand, the transfer of technology to a supplier, which improves that supplier's quality and/or efficiency, may be appropriate and may pay big dividends as the resulting improvements are realized through the value chain. On the other hand, to the extent that the technology transferred includes process knowhow, product design insight, and/or proprietary features information, the outcome could be less welcome—even disastrous! There are three general areas that require careful consideration and evaluation during these sourcing deliberations.

Intellectual Property Rights Sensitivity. As previously discussed, formal agreement with suppliers on intellectual proprietary rights is critically important and has strategic consequences. This concept will appear self-evident to those firms in high-technology industries. Typically, "high-tech" firms have established formal policies and procedures in this area. However, *all* manufacturing and service firms must include intellectual and proprietary rights considerations in their sourcing strategy evaluation criteria.

As an example, a large service company in the transportation industry recently designed an innovative fix to a long-standing and troublesome coupling device. The new design not only significantly reduces maintenance time and expense, but also measurably improves loading and unloading efficiency. The new design was sourced without restrictions and the firm's standard terms and conditions were silent on proprietary rights, make and have made licenses, and so forth. Additionally, the firm did not have a culture that was sensitive to patent protection type issues since it was a service firm and typically did not design products. *As a result, the innovative device is now an industry standard and does not provide a proprietary competitive advantage to its designer.*

Cooperation Scope Sensitivity. Throughout the book, the considerable opportunities available through improved and trusting relationships with selected suppliers are emphasized. Notwithstanding the total commitment to these AKT relationships, an attempt has been made to present a balanced approach. The AKT relationships outlined are the result of extensive research and serious strategic consideration. A firm's strategic decision to cooperate in one area of business or on a specific project must not imply that the parties to the AKT alliance share data, technology, market information, product plans, and/or process knowhow *beyond the scope* of the specific and limited focus of their joint project agreement. Considerable discipline is required to ensure that the members of cross-functional teams from both firms focus their discussions and limit their activity to the project(s) that have been approved for joint consideration. International sourcing alliances represent a particularly important challenge since the business customs vary between nations. Through painful experience, American executives have learned that some international firms have developed aggressive technology transfer cultures and reputations.[a]

Strategic Capabilities and Intent Analysis. Consideration must be given to the long-term business intentions of each of the supplier candidates as part of any sourcing strategy analysis. Typically, this is not difficult to evaluate. Many potential suppliers may already be competitors at some level, either directly or indirectly. Other supplier candidates may have formally announced their business interests or they may have otherwise indicated their intentions through a pattern of business activity. Sourcing important requirements and sharing important technology with a competitor or potential competitor may be the best possible alternative. Many "competitors" appear to be joining in business relationships these days: IBM and Apple Computer, Ford Motor Company and Nissan, Siemens and IBM, and so on. However, there is very little sympathy for the long litany of firms that have lost significant market share to one-time suppliers who decided to for-

---

[a]For a shocking article addressing one U.S. firm's abusive treatment in this area, see "Patent Protection or Piracy—A CEO Views Japan," by Donald M. Spero, *Harvard Business Review* (September–October, 1990).

ward integrate. America has lost entire industries (television, stereos, clothing, etc.) and significant portions of other industries (semiconductors, shoes, and machine tools) as the direct result of poorly thought out sourcing activities that all but put suppliers in direct competition with their customers. Supplier selection and sourcing decisions must be treated and handled as strategic issues of the highest order.

COMPETITIVE PRACTICES STRATEGY

As discussed earlier, the use of competitive bidding will be significantly reduced in the American Keiretsu environment. Therefore, ensuring the competitive cost of purchased inputs becomes an important strategic concern. Cost management and control have a direct impact on a firm's ability to sustain its global competitive position. One of the often debated drawbacks of vertical integration involves cost control. Many have argued that captive divisions eventually lose their competitive position as a result of the absence of competition and weaknesses in cost accounting and allocation systems. Additionally, the absence of outside customers and suppliers eliminates vital stimuli forcing technological growth. Many authorities attribute General Motors, IBM, and N.V. Philips' recent decline to a combination of these issues.[b]

Given this history, questions have been raised regarding the effectiveness of supplier partnership-like relations, alliances, and so forth. These questions are important and prudent. Indeed, any firm interested in implementing the concepts outlined in this book must first establish organizational expertise in total-cost management using the techniques outlined in Chapter 7.

---

[b]For an expanded debate on the issue of vertical integration, see Ted Kumpe and Piet T. Bolwijn's article, "Manufacturing: The New Case for Vertical Integration," *Harvard Business Review* (March–April, 1988), pp. 75–81, and our letter to the editor of the *Harvard Business Review*, printed in the March–April 1989 issue, pp. 190–194.

There are three important principles that provide the basis of a formal competitive practices strategy. The first is a commitment to measure total cost. The firm must not be distracted by price levels, purchase-price variance reports, and other partial cost reporting data so common in today's accounting-focused reporting systems.

The second principle involves an acknowledgement of the importance of the supplier's profit margin. Suppliers must be allowed the opportunity to earn appropriate profits, given their industry. This is necessary to attract investment, fund future growth, and contribute to the value chain's future success. The buying firm must not assume a responsibility for the supplier's profits. However, the buying firm also must not profit at the supplier's expense. Supplier turnover is even more costly than employee turnover and needs to be managed.

The third principle is closely related with the second. Each AKT relationship must develop a culture that drives and measures continuous joint cost-reduction efforts. The global competitive market is dynamic. Economic pressures constantly drive innovation and these pressures must be encouraged and acknowledged. Market pressures force competitive innovation and continuous improvement. AKT relationships must not become safe havens from which one side can derive increased profits and market share at the expense of the other or from the competitiveness of the value chain.

Specific competitive practices will need to be developed for each supply industry and possibly each AKT relationship. To the extent possible, these strategies should be cost based. Obviously, cost-based pricing is easier in some industries like stampings, forgings, plastic molding, and so forth, than it is in other industries such as semiconductors, engineering test equipment, and so on. Each situation is unique. The goal, however, is to have an agreement, developed by both firms, that not only identifies cost elements, but also establishes cost-accounting processes that set purchase prices. Additionally, formal volume and/or time triggers should be set that will drive continuous reevaluation of costs so that both parties have the opportunity to monitor this important financial aspect of the relationship.

MANAGEMENT INFORMATION STRATEGY

The development of thorough Supply Management strategies requires knowledgeable individuals, sound analysis, and considerable data research. The effectiveness of the current Procurement Process, inventory management, individual suppliers, and carriers must be evaluated. The required research must be completed to form a baseline understanding.

With limited exceptions, the management information systems available to evaluate Procurement Process, inventory management, suppliers, and carriers' effectiveness are marginal, at best. Typically, standard cost data are being captured and stored for analysis. These data serve the accounting and finance needs of firms quite well, but have limited value to Purchasing. Historical trend data are often not easily sorted by component usage, price, sourcing, inventory performance, and/or delivery and quality performance. Many firms do not maintain such data for more than one year.

Firms interested in initiatives aimed at evaluation and implementation of AKT concepts may have to start with an assessment of their current management information systems. Many multibillion-dollar firms literally do not know what they purchase by supplier, item purchased, price, or shipment *for the current year*, let alone for the past five years. Meaningful activity records that provide sourcing patterns, pricing history (not standard cost), inventory activity, and inbound freight are essential for the research and analysis required to support the strategic planning process. Reconstructing these data is costly and time-consuming. However, if the firm's management information system has not captured or retained detailed activity data, executives are left with little choice. As previously noted, if total costs are to be measured, the firm's management information system must also capture the costs involved in scrap, re-work, process yield losses, and field costs that result from defective purchased materials.

SUPPLY BASE STRATEGY

By the year 2000, achieving excellence will no longer be sufficient; success will depend on being a valued member of a successful value chain.

The supply base strategy concept starts with two basic assumptions. First, America's long-accepted practice of supplier selection, the invisible hand of Adam Smith aided by three bids and a cloud of dust, produces random results. Second, very few American firms view sourcing as a strategic activity.

One reason for the Japanese keiretsu's superior results is that *the sourcing process was designed with "malice of forethought" to select suppliers based on a strategic criterion. American industry, on the other hand, has never asked its sourcing activity to provide strategic results.* The task has generally been to acquire current requirements at the lowest purchase price, with little regard for "all-in-cost," total cost, or very much else. If one wishes to test this statement on his or her firm's current practice, he or she should find out if the firm formally measures and reports "purchase price variance." If the answer is yes, chances are buyers are price buyers, regardless of claims to the contrary. *Management gets what it measures!*

The development of a firm's supply base strategy involves a selection process driven by specific criteria for quality, cost management, technology access, and so forth. The development of the criteria and the selection process itself is a higher-order executive activity equal in every way to the development of the firm's marketing strategy. This activity requires cross-functional involvement, talented and experienced resources, a formal supply base monitoring system, and the regular and frequent review and participation of top management. It is simply unreasonable to assume that any firm can achieve World Class status without World Class suppliers. The competition for World Class suppliers has already begun. The firm's supply base strategy must identify specific needs, match those needs with outstanding suppliers, and develop measurement criteria to drive continuous improvement. Through this process, sourcing becomes strategic selection, the supply base is reduced, and the desired improvements in quality, time, and technology access are realized.

Monitoring the Supply Environment

In order to develop appropriate corporate and supply strategies, a company must be aware of its supply environment just as it must be aware of its customer environment. The supply environment includes all those activities that are relevant to the company, to its suppliers, and to those who supply its suppliers. The process of monitoring the supply environment includes tracking political, economic, technological, social, and regulatory trends. In addition, competitor activities, existing supplier activities, supply market size, and potential supplier activities should be tracked. Decisions as to which specific trends need monitoring should be made by a team that includes Purchasing, engineering, manufacturing, or other concerned members of the Supply Management team.

A proactive supply environmental scan must be performed. It must attempt to predict the supply environment into the future. It should be a structured and deliberate effort. Specific information should be collected and a pre-established methodology should be used. The strategic scan is searching for competitive advantage. Appendix A includes, among others, several questions that must be addressed in this critical area.[c]

Identifying Time Bombs

An important byproduct of supply base strategy analysis is the identification of "time bombs" that require timely action to "defuse." Figure 4-4 portrays the relationship between the criticality of a component, service, or material and the mutual value of the relationship to both the buyer and the supplier. An example may clarify these interdependent relations. A selected component and the relationship with the selected supplier may both be critical to the buying firm. However, if the component manufacturer chooses to deal on an arm's-length basis, indicating that the relationship is of relatively low value to the component supplier, a "time bomb" exists. The buying firm must take timely action, either to move the relationship to one of mutual value or to resource with a World Class supplier willing to enter into an AKT alliance. This method of evaluating purchase requirements against mutual relationship value also provides necessary information about the positioning of all purchased inputs. This information is required in the development of the formal supply base strategy and the subsequent implementation activities.

ALLIANCE AND RELATIONSHIP STRATEGY

The business press has been full of articles and texts outlining the many advantages of business alliances. Several recent and noteworthy works include:

---

[c] The interested reader is urged to read *Purchasing: Principles & Management* by Peter Baily and David Farmer for more insight into this topic.[4]

- "The Way to Win in Cross-Border Alliances," by Joel Bleeke & David Ernst, *Harvard Business Review* (November–December 1991), pp.127–135.
- "Novellus: Thriving—With a Little Help from Its Friends," by Robert D. Hof, *Business Week* (January 27, 1992), p. 60.
- *Partnerships for Profit: Structuring and Managing Strategic Alliances*, by Jordan D. Lewis (New York: Free Press, 1990).
- *The Practical Guide to Joint Ventures & Corporate Alliances*, by Robert Porter Lynch (New York: John Wiley, 1990).
- "The Partners," *Business Week*, Cover Story (February 10, 1992).

FIGURE 4–4
Criticality/Sourcing Interaction

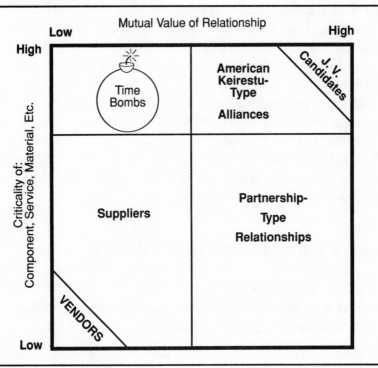

To date, the published work typically approaches the importance of alliances from a downstream (marketing) point of view. Equity participation between the alliance partners is frequently involved in the examples cited. Many of the alliance examples provided in the literature appear to parallel the equity partnerships so common in the Japanese keiretsu structures. No exception is taken with any of these writings; however, some clarification of terms appears to be required. Alliances involving equity sharing are more appropriately referred to as joint ventures, equity sharing partnerships, or joint operating agreements. For our purposes, supplier alliance agreements do not involve equity. These agreements are strategic supply agreements negotiated between buyers and sellers based on a common commitment to continuous improvement through time. The intention of the parties is that the sourcing commitment is permanent as long as the needs of both parties are being met. Only extraordinary circumstances could cause re-sourcing action and then, only after considerable corrective action by professionals from both firms and the personal involvement of both COOs. These agreements offer all the advantages discussed in the cited literature but suffer considerably less business risk if developed and negotiated with the due diligence outlined in *The American Keiretsu*.

The strategic advantages documented in the referenced literature are equally powerful and actually implemented more easily from a reverse point of view: that is, *customer-driven supplier alliances versus supplier-driven customer alliances*. While this may at first seem to be a play on words, it is not, and the difference is noteworthy.

Managers typically view the proactive approaches to alliances taken by marketing organizations to be the "natural" order of things. Our recommendation, however, is that the American Keiretsu concepts drive strategic Supply Management implementation and assume an aggressive, proactive approach to alliances as well. The buying firm is much better positioned to identify, quantify, document, and achieve the available efficiencies through alliance opportunities. The current legal structure in the United States also favors a leadership position for the buyer in formulating alliance-type structures. Antitrust laws provide much greater latitude for the buyer than they do for the seller. As an example, bundling is illegal for sellers to practice or suggest; however, buyers are free of such restrictions.

There is a tremendous opportunity available for organizations to develop a new paradigm for the strategic management of purchased inputs. At the majority of firms, expenditures for outsourced materials, services, and equipment represent well over 50 percent of revenues. The strategic approach outlined can generate stunning improvements. Most of the advantages identified, and often complained about in the Japanese keiretsu, are available to American companies. America can't copy the Japanese keiretsu directly, nor should it; however, America can achieve superior results through a combination of the best of the Japanese vertical keiretsu with the best of American entrepreneurship.

CONCLUDING REMARKS

A successful firm's supply strategy must be integrated with the goals, objectives, and strategies of the firm. This supply strategy is at the heart of any successful strategic Supply Management effort. AKT relationships, in turn, are based on a logical outcome of this successful Supply Management effort.

The next five chapters focus on the Procurement Process, an essential foundation of strategic Supply Management and of AKT relationships.

NOTES

1. Robert Reich, *Fortune Magazine* (May 18, 1992), p. 98.
2. The interested reader is referred to the article "Fundamentals of Strategic Supply Management" by Michael F. Doyle, *Purchasing World* (December 1991).
3. "Warns of Japanese CPU 'Control,' " *Computer News* (April 13, 1981).
4. Peter Baily and David Farmer, *Purchasing: Principles and Management*, 6th ed. (London, U.K.: Pitman Publishing, 1990).

CHAPTER 5

BRINGING QUALITY PRODUCTS TO MARKET QUICKLY

The Atlas Door Company's strategy, which proved remarkably successful, was to respond to customer needs for special doors faster than competition. A critical part of this strategy was the selection of key suppliers that could respond to these tight customer time requirements. The firm's pre-tax earnings have been 20 percent of sales, which is about five times the industry average.[1]

Joel Goldschein

Global competitors are embracing simultaneous or concurrent engineering involving supply partners in order to upgrade product and service quality while reducing the time-to-market. The ultimate benefits result when selected American Keiretsu-type (AKT) suppliers are involved.

World Class manufacturers recognize that many functions must play active roles during the development of new products: product engineers; research technologists; quality, reliability, and manufacturing engineers; operations; marketing; customer service; *supply managers and selected suppliers* (see Figure 5-1).[a] Early involvement of Purchasing and selected suppliers improves product quality and reliability while compressing development time and reducing total material cost.[2] Purchasing and selected sup-

---

[a] It is also noted that several World Class organizations include their customers at several stages of new product development.

FIGURE 5–1
The Fully Enhanced Development Team

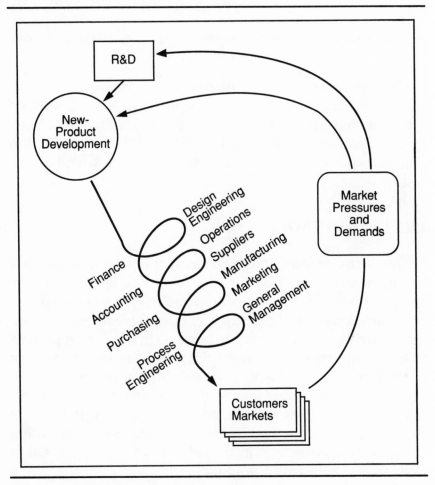

pliers contribute their technical expertise and knowledge of outside manufacturing and quality capabilities while simultaneously addressing commercial issues.

" . . . in order to involve the supplier network in the innovation activity, the lead customer has to create two interdependent incentive systems:

- designing and implementing a supply management approach for the involvement of suppliers in the current development activity;
- creating an incentive system for the long-term alignment of the technology strategy of suppliers."[3]

This chapter examines the role of the American Keiretsu as it is applied to the product development process. Emphasis is placed on the roles of the firm's Supply Management function and selected suppliers. It is noted that nonproduction requirements will be addressed specifically in Chapter 8.

THE DESIGN PROCESS

Design is the progression of an abstract notion to something having function and fixed form. The desired levels of quality and reliability must be engineered in during the design phase of the new product. "The supplier must have access to product design as early as humanly possible in the design process to assure optimal use of any special skills or processes they can contribute."[4] *The design stage is also the optimum point at which the vast majority of the cost of making an item can be reduced or controlled.* If costs are not minimized during the design stage, excessive cost may be built in permanently, resulting in expensive, possibly noncompetitive, products that fail to fully realize their profit potential.

These days, one hears a great deal about designing for manufacturability; however, invariably, the focus is the firm's *internal* manufacturing process. But when those responsible for design ignore the manufacturing and technological capabilities *of outside suppliers*, problems with quality, time-to-market, configuration, and cost are the inevitable result. If optimum design performance is to be achieved, suppliers must be active from the beginning, when they can have a major impact on performance, time, and cost. Selected suppliers should participate in feasibility studies, value engineering, and in prototype, failure, and stress analysis, among other product development tasks.

There is a growing trend among manufacturers such as Toyota and, more recently, Chrysler to develop an "envelope" of performance specifications for suppliers. The suppliers' engineering and CAD/CAM tools, not the customer firm's, are then dedicated to designing selected components. This approach allows engineers at the customer firm to focus on the development of more sophisticated core technologies and proprietary systems. The customer firm's engineers do not prepare blueprints for nonstrategic components. However, they review and approve the supplier's designs. Such action not only redirects critical engineering resources to higher value activities, but places responsibility for manufacturability and quality with the supplier.

> The platform team, long the standard way of putting cars together among Japanese auto makers, has been officially embraced by Chrysler executives as superior to the compartmentalized "chimney" system still prevalent throughout the U.S. industry. But while each of the Big Three U.S. auto makers has experimented with teams, they have been slow to adopt the seemingly alien system wholesale.
>
> The point of the platform team is simplification: When designers, product engineers, manufacturing engineers, purchasing agents, suppliers, and line workers make decisions together from the beginning, it saves time, money, and untold hassle when the car finally hits the assembly line.
>
> But at the same time, the team system introduces to product development the unpredictable element of human relations—a wild card far more complex than engineering and assembling the 2,600 parts of a car.[5]

In order to involve suppliers effectively and early, manufacturing companies should invite selected suppliers' engineers into their own engineering departments. (Co-location of key supplier company engineers has long been practiced in Japanese industry.) Manufacturers should allow key suppliers to review the design of the entire subassembly before committing to it. Not only does this tease out new ideas but it also helps the supply partner understand the customer's real needs—and likely future needs.

As an example, a major original equipment manufacturer (OEM) assigned an engineer to design a metal bracket for a shock mounting device. The engineer designed the bracket as partially shown in Figure 5-2(a). The Purchasing department sourced the bracket to an eager stamping supplier and approved the hundred thousand dollars required for tooling.

The supplier was never able to produce parts to print. Much worse, the .15 inch diameter hole punches would explode from time to time, causing a serious safety hazard. After over a year of finger pointing, the OEM finally accepted the feasibility concern that the supplier had raised originally: it is not possible to punch a hole through a piece of steel consistently when the diameter of the hole is smaller than the thickness of the steel. The corrected design is partially shown in Figure 5-2(b). This design approach holds the critical center position of each hole but provides slots that can consistently be stamped safely to specification.

Some engineers without specific training or experience in stamping design would not realize this specific technical design issue. *Every field of design engineering has special design criteria of this nature. No engineer can be expected to know all the technical nuances that have developed through time in every field of technology.*

> At Tennant we have found that involving our suppliers at the design stage has improved our products. Since they are the experts in their fields, they prevent us from making mistakes, help us save money and time, and help us do it right the first time.[6]

The changing competitive environment forces much more planning, coordination, and review to take place during

FIGURE 5-2
Bracket Design Example

a. Sketch of bracket as originally designed by the OEM

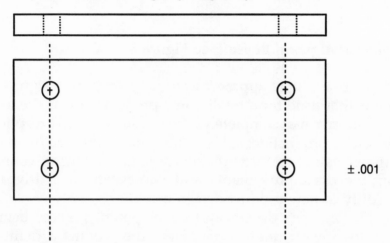

b. Sketch of same bracket as redesigned by the stamping supplier

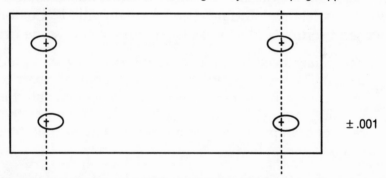

the design and development process than previously was the case. Complexity of product lines must be addressed. Lower levels of complexity result in higher schedule stability, a necessary prerequisite to just-in-time (JIT) manufacturing. Feasibility studies, computer simulations, prototype analysis, failure analyses, stress analyses, and value engineering all must be conducted in an effort to develop *producible*, defect-free products quickly.

The new product development process has undergone a tremendous change during the past few years. The process is described in Figures 5–3 (a), (b), and (c) and discussed below.

The Investigation Phase (See Figure 5–3 (a))

There are multiple approaches to new product design. The first is that used for a totally new product. This is the least used approach as completely new products are an exception. Most new product design is actually an adaptation or an expanded feature set for a previous design. Advancing technology, process improvements, and market expansion drive the majority of new product design activity.

The modern design and development process begins with the investigation phase. First, the product is defined. This function is normally performed with considerable marketing involvement and has been formally titled "Customer Focused Product and Process Development" at some firms.

> Companies need to incorporate the customer into product design. That means getting more and more members of an organization in contact with the customer—manufacturing and design people, as well as sales and marketing staff. You can, for example, have customers sitting in on your internal committee meetings.[7]

Next, the attributes, desires, and objectives for the product are established. These attributes are based on marketing's perception or knowledge of what customers want, balanced against the company's objectives and resources. Products that are potentially compatible with the firm's objectives (profit potential, sales volume, payback period, etc.) and resources (personnel, machines, and management) are considered for development. Product objectives, including performance, price, quality, and market availability, are then established and become the criteria that guide subsequent

FIGURE 5–3
The Modern Design and Development Process

a. Investigation Phase

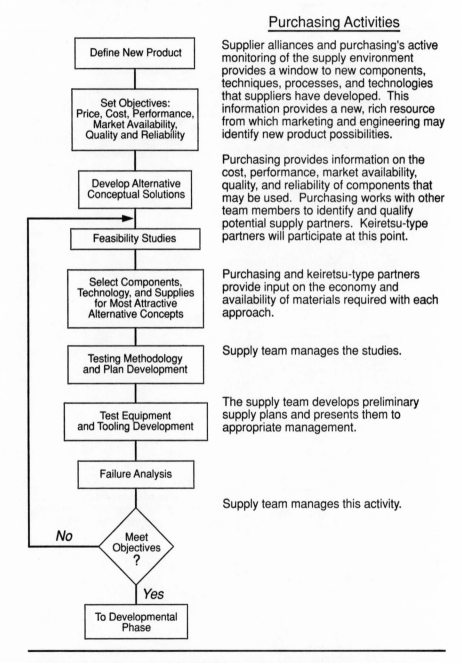

Purchasing Activities

Supplier alliances and purchasing's active monitoring of the supply environment provides a window to new components, techniques, processes, and technologies that suppliers have developed. This information provides a new, rich resource from which marketing and engineering may identify new product possibilities.

Purchasing provides information on the cost, performance, market availability, quality, and reliability of components that may be used. Purchasing works with other team members to identify and qualify potential supply partners. Keiretsu-type partners will participate at this point.

Purchasing and keiretsu-type partners provide input on the economy and availability of materials required with each approach.

Supply team manages the studies.

The supply team develops preliminary supply plans and presents them to appropriate management.

Supply team manages this activity.

Source: Adapted from David Burt, *Proactive Procurement: The Key to Increased Profits, Productivity, and Quality* (Englewood Cliffs, N.J.: Prentice Hall, Inc., 1984).

FIGURE 5–3 (continued)

b. Development Phase

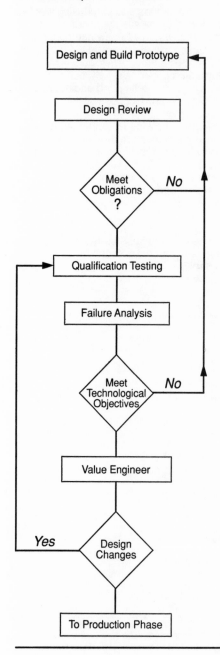

Purchasing Activities

Supply team manages procurement of prototype requirements from production sources.

Supply team reviews for cost, timing, feasibility, and standardization.

Supply team provides input on cost and availability of alternative designs, processes, and materials.

FIGURE 5–3 (*continued*)

c. Production Phase

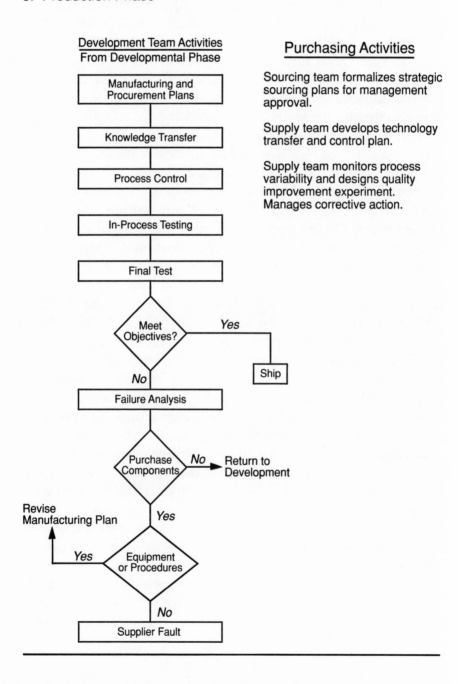

Development Team Activities
From Developmental Phase

- Manufacturing and Procurement Plans
- Knowledge Transfer
- Process Control
- In-Process Testing
- Final Test

Meet Objectives? — *Yes* → Ship

No

- Failure Analysis

Purchase Components — *No* → Return to Development

Yes

Revise Manufacturing Plan ← *Yes* — Equipment or Procedures

No

- Supplier Fault

Purchasing Activities

Sourcing team formalizes strategic sourcing plans for management approval.

Supply team develops technology transfer and control plan.

Supply team monitors process variability and designs quality improvement experiment. Manages corrective action.

design, planning, distribution channels selection, and decision making.

The planned product life cycle typically includes not only the original product but several planned future products that will incorporate improvements in design, function, features, and so on. These new products are driven by advances in technology, design, and/or materials; competitive offerings; and customer expectations. These desired advances are most commonly known at the time of the original product design, but they are not included in the design, as the technology does not exist, or requires additional development to be production ready. This product feature design "wish list" is very important to the design engineer as he or she most closely understands the design trade-offs and compromises that were included in the original design. This "wish list" of technology requirements is extremely important. Unfortunately, most firms do not document these technical interests that eventually drive their product development process. Not only should these data be documented but they must become an important focus for the supply partner R&D efforts since quick development will drive new product offerings that add additional sales volume, frequently at premium sales prices.

As shown in Figure 5-3 (a), alternative ways of satisfying these needs, desires, and objectives should be developed and evaluated against the criteria. Several options may meet engineering's constraints while offering a wide range of cost, availability, and reliability choices. Purchasing personnel and selected suppliers provide information on the availability of the materials and subassemblies to be purchased under each approach.

The early involvement of quality engineers allows advanced quality planning to commence in a timely manner. Quality standards are developed to ensure that components and products being designed can be produced at the quality specified. Specifications for test equipment and test procedures are also developed at this time. Required test equipment is then designed, sourced, and manufactured. Each supplier's quality management system must be reviewed to ensure that once production begins on these components, defect-free materials will result.

The selection of required standard components is facilitated by the availability of a current internal catalog of standard items and sources which have been prequalified.[b] The use of such a catalog simplifies the design engineers' job while simultaneously supporting the efforts of materials management to standardize the items used. The use of standard materials, production processes, and methods shortens the design time and lowers the cost of designing and producing an item. In addition, standardization reduces quality problems with incoming materials, inventories, administrative expenses, inspection, and handling expenses, while obtaining lower unit costs.

As shown in Figure 5–3 (a), the selection of technologies is a complex issue due to inherent cost/benefits trade-offs and functional orientations. Engineers are eager to incorporate the latest technology. The marketplace often richly rewards those who are first to market with innovative products; therefore, there is a strong case for incorporating new technology or processes before they are perfected.

But the cost of such a decision can be high. Not only does such an approach result in a proliferation of components to be purchased and stocked, but it frequently results in the use of items whose production processes have not yet stabilized: quality problems, production disruptions, and delays frequently result, all increasing project risk. Engineering, quality, Purchasing, and manufacturing personnel must ensure that both the costs and benefits of such advanced develop-

---

[b]This catalog is developed and maintained by the joint efforts of engineering, reliability engineering, Purchasing, and manufacturing engineering. It is a result of a team effort that considers the technical and commercial implications of the items included. The internal catalog is in contrast to a supplier's catalog, which, while simplifying the engineer's efforts to describe an item, places the firm in an unintentional sole-source posture.

ments are properly considered. The design team should design new products to the requirements of the customer, not necessarily to the state-of-the-art.

When a component or subsystem is to be developed by an outside supplier and an AKT supplier has not been selected, one or more carefully prequalified potential suppliers may be asked to develop design proposals for the required item. If an AKT relationship has been established for a particular component, only this supplier will be involved. Potential suppliers are given performance, cost, weight, and reliability objectives and are provided information on how and where the item will fit and/or function in the larger system. These potential suppliers must develop quality plans during the design of the item to ensure that the item will be producible at the quality specified. Selection of the "winning" supplier design proposal is a team effort with Purchasing, design engineering, reliability engineering, product planning, quality, manufacturing, finance, and field support participating. Performance, quality, reliability, and cost are all considered.

Development Phase

The rapid advance in computer technology and software have made the feasibility of large-scale, complex computer simulations possible. Manufacturers typically conduct extensive computer simulation to identify interferences, fit issues, functionality, algorithmic logic accuracy, and so forth, prior to the development of prototypes. As the technology continues to advance, computer modeling and simulation may replace prototype development.

Notwithstanding these technical advances, breadboard and/or hardware prototypes frequently are developed so that the design team may conduct tests on the integrated system to eliminate performance and quality problems. The selected approach is reviewed in detail for feasibility and likely risk. Efforts are taken to reduce risk to acceptable levels by developing and testing prototypes.

Following the model in Figure 5-3 (b), the first complete prototypes of the new product are designed, built, and tested. Documentation such as material lists, drawings, and test procedures is created. It is not unusual to repeat this phase more than once, perhaps building the first prototype in the laboratory to test the design and the second generation in manufacturing as a test of the documentation. The design should not leave this phase until a prototype has met all the design goals, although it may not be possible to demonstrate the reliability goal because of the small number of prototypes available to test.

Frequent design reviews are scheduled so that the new design and the project process can be measured, compared to previously established objectives, and improved. Purchasing and selected suppliers participate in these design reviews and provide information on the effect of specifications and the design status of required materials. The buyer, along with selected suppliers, must ensure that specifications and functional descriptions are complete, unambiguous, and provide the necessary information on how purchased items are to be checked or tested. The buyer must be satisfied that all purchase item specifications are written in terms relevant to and understandable by the potential suppliers.

Value engineering (VE) techniques are applied to improve quality and reduce cost throughout the design process. Selected suppliers work directly with the design team and actively contribute to the VE process. Leading-edge firms such as General Electric Medical Systems conduct a "producibility review" as part of their VE process.[9]

The Production Phase (See Figure 5-3 (c))

In the production phase, the manufacturing plan and the procurement plan are finalized and implemented. As a result of early involvement, Purchasing has developed formal written procurement project plans that have been reviewed and approved by senior management. Purchasing has worked with selected suppliers and design engineering to develop the appropriate specification. The approved plans must be implemented in a timely manner consistent with production planning and tooling lead-time requirements.

Management of Engineering Changes

Engineering changes require formal control and discipline. The optimization of product development time, quality, and cost demands that the supplier be actively involved in managing and coordinating required changes. All design and manufacturing process changes must be controlled, both in-house and at suppliers. Any changes in components, processes, or the product itself may have profound impacts on quality, cost, performance, appearance, and acceptability in the marketplace. Changes, especially at the component or subassembly level, can have a major effect on manufacturing and quality. Frequently, there is pressure to make problem-driven (i.e., poor performance, early failures, and safety hazards) design changes quickly. These problems are often the result of inadequate simulation or prototype tests. Design changes made as a result of such pressure often create unforeseen problems. If changes to the configuration and manufacturing process of an item are not controlled, the manufacturer will experience variability that can seriously affect quality and reliability and eventually compromise the integrity of the product. Inventories of materials will require needlessly expensive re-work, control, and segregation to be adapted to the new configuration. Some materials may not be able to be reworked and must be scrapped. Quite obviously, this monumental task is greatly simplified with a focused, consolidated, committed supply base such as results under the American Keiretsu concepts and techniques.

Adherence to this or a similar design process is a key prerequisite to the firm's development and introduction of successful new products in a minimum of time. Product quality, cost, and availability all must receive proper attention. As seen, engineering, manufacturing, marketing, quality, and Purchasing and *suppliers* all have vital roles to play in the design process.

QUALITY

In addition to designing in quality during the design process, the new product development team must also review the quality system to ensure quality, both by suppliers and by internal operations.

The design of experiments, as described by our colleague Keki Bhote in his wonderful book, *World Class Quality,*[10] should be considered both by the design team and by suppliers. This powerful approach to avoiding problems during design and identifying the source of problems during manufacture is an essential element of total quality management.

During a recent discussion with the CEO of a major supplier to both American and Japanese firms, the question was asked, "Are you employing DOE (design of experiments)?" "We sure are," he replied. "It was forced on us by one of our customers. But they will never have to force us again. We saved so much time and avoided so many problems, both in design and in manufacture, that it's now part of our standard operating procedure!"

As firms and their suppliers design their quality systems for the new product and its components, test and inspection equipment must be addressed. All too frequently, such action is overlooked until too late, with significant quality problems resulting.

APPLYING THE AKT SUPPLY CONCEPT

Applying AKT concepts at the project level takes place in parallel with the development of a new (or upgraded) product. The Procurement Process at this level is facilitated by the strategic supply initiative.

The Project Team's Role in Product Development

Chapter 3 introduced the role of the cross-functional team in Supply Management. During product development, it is recommended that a dedicated project team be established to carry out the required tasks. The team members are responsible for specific activities required to bring the product to production.

> Design is not the province of engineering, not even of engineering and manufacturing jointly. Instead, representatives of every stage in a product's life cycle, from materials employed in its manufacture to its ultimate disposal, participate in setting its design specification.[11]

Figure 5–4 is introduced with two objectives. First, it shows representative project activities and organizational functions that are typically involved. Second, Figure 5–4 can be used as an organizational planning worksheet to aid in the development of the new product development team and team member assignments.[c]

Ideally, the engineering project team will have considerable overlap with the cross-functional team responsible for ensuring that the supplier is World Class (see Chapter 6) and for developing new and updated products. Development, operations, quality, and Purchasing managers who will have day-to-day responsibility for the relationship should also be involved in business negotiations. The team members must meet, identify, and agree on their needs, objectives, priorities, milestones, and performance measures prior to meeting with their supplier counterparts. Figure 5–5 lists some selected sample objectives that must be considered in the devel-

---

[c]For a thorough review of project cross-functional team organization, see pages 111 through 117 of *Beyond Negotiation*, cited in the endnotes.

FIGURE 5–4
Pro Forma Requirements Planning Worksheet

Project Activities

Organizational Function:	Technology	New Product Ideas	Establish Objectives	Product Design	Reliability Design	Test Plan	Failure Engineering	Specification Analysis	Supplier Selection	Design Development	Standardization Reviews	Value Engineering	Technology Control	Other
Design Engineering														
Marketing														
Customers														
Process Engineering														
Quality														
Purchasing														
Suppliers														
Manufacturing														
Customer Service														
Finance														
Other														

Legend:
● Fully Involved
○ Partially Involved

opment of project specific plans. Figure 5–6 shows a sample project planning and control methodology that may be of value to the cross-functional teams.

Trust

All members of the firm, and especially the project team members, must ensure that they not misrepresent any fact. They must work to ensure the other party's full understanding and they must check for this understanding. Such an approach to communication lays the foundation for trust and sound, long-lasting relationships.

FIGURE 5–5
Sample Objectives

American Keiretsu Project Specific Agreements should include:
- Performance and critical characteristics identification.
- Project timing (milestones) commitments and plans.
- Resource commitments.
- Quantities, schedules, and capacity data by operation.
- Specifications/tests and test methodology agreement.
- Product safety considerations.
- Quality advances throughout the product's life cycle.
- Price and costs evaluation, control, and reporting.
- Process and other improvements throughout the product's life cycle.
- Service support and rollout plans.
- Quality plan (including DOE, SPC, CpK, and variables data collection and reporting).
- Operational and administrative procedures.
- Ordering procedures.
- Contingency plans.
- Recycling considerations (disposal, environmental issues, etc.).

Osamu Nobuto, President of Mazda, in his December 1987 remarks to Ford Motor Company commented:

> With American suppliers, we start at the top of the organization and receive very nice words and promises from the management. Then we find that as the project goes along, we are dealing with people much further down in the organization who do not really understand or have the ability to realize the promises. In addition, there is often a lack of consistent assignment of personnel at each phase, with insufficient communication from one phase to another.[12]

The success of the specific project and of the AKT relationship depends as much (or more) on trust and mutual commitment as on anything the parties can put on paper. Without high levels of trust, the venture is doomed. *Based on*

FIGURE 5–6
Planning/Progress Chart

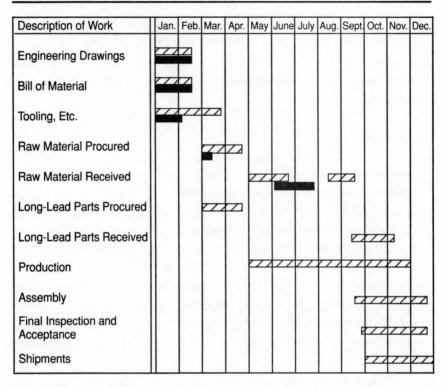

Description of Work	Jan.	Feb.	Mar.	Apr.	May	June	July	Aug.	Sept.	Oct.	Nov.	Dec.
Engineering Drawings												
Bill of Material												
Tooling, Etc.												
Raw Material Procured												
Raw Material Received												
Long-Lead Parts Procured												
Long-Lead Parts Received												
Production												
Assembly												
Final Inspection and Acceptance												
Shipments												

Key: Planned ▨▨▨▨
       Actual ■■■■■

the crucial role of trust, it is strongly recommended that personnel from both the buying firm and supplier participate in trust-building exercises.

DEVELOPING THE PROJECT BUSINESS PLAN

It is essential that both parties represent their project needs, objectives, and concerns in an atmosphere of openness. Obviously, both parties are concerned with their own firm's best interests. But their focus must be on enlarging the pie for both parties, not on redistributing the current one. Each project must be developed as a stand-alone opportunity complete with its own business plan. Both parties must view the project as worthwhile and profitable in its own right. The project focus helps drive common interests and is another key to success.

Lawyers

Typically, lawyers are not involved in the face-to-face discussions. However, it is recommended that attorneys follow each project, review draft business plans, and ask hard questions about commitments, contingencies, and, especially, intellectual property rights. An attorney's probing questions can expose weaknesses in the team's understandings. AKT relationships do not fail due to poorly written contracts. They fail (or fail to reach their full potential) because of misunderstandings among the parties or because managers from the appropriate functional areas fail to support implementation fully.

Based on the special relationship between the AKT parties, a short agreement outlining the project and referencing the umbrella agreement may be issued in lieu of a standard purchase order. The focus is cooperation, trust, and synergism, not possible litigation; however, this approach must not encourage careless business practices.

TECHNICAL SKILLS REQUIRED OF SUPPLY MANAGEMENT PROFESSIONALS

Recently, while talking with the supply manager at a division of a major computer manufacturer, the manager addressed an essential evolution in focus and staffing in his supply operation: "Our heritage has been the management of materials. Our future is up front in design."

In order to be contributors during the design process, Supply Management professionals must possess sufficient technical (engineering, chemistry, quality, manufacturing, etc.) skills to understand the processes, to communicate successfully with their technical colleagues, and to motivate or persuade them to consider the commercial and supply base issues involved.

Two successful approaches to this staffing and human resource issue are popular: (1) hire people with technical backgrounds for key Supply Management jobs and then provide the necessary Supply Management training, or (2) provide the necessary technical training for present and/or potential Supply Management professionals. Seeing this need, in 1992, Western Michigan University introduced a new undergraduate interdisciplinary degree program in Supply Management, offered jointly by the School of Business and the College of Engineering.

Recognizing the importance of Supply Management to its success, a major Japanese manufacturer began grooming its present vice president of supply some 15 years before he assumed this position. During the mid 1970s, this individual, a graduate of an excellent engineering school, was sponsored by his employer to obtain his MBA (with an emphasis on Supply Management) at a leading U.S. university. After receiving his MBA, the future vice president of supply worked at a number of career-broadening assignments prior to being promoted to his present position.

The majority of new hires into Supply Management at General Electric's major appliance group in Louisville, Ky., possess an undergraduate degree in engineering and an MBA. Polaroid has a Ph.D. in chemistry on its Purchasing staff. Delco Electronics details promising engineers for tours in Purchasing. In fact, the vast majority of Delco buyers and Purchasing managers are trained engineers. These and other firms have learned the importance of having technically qualified personnel in Supply Management!

CONCLUDING REMARKS

Simultaneous or concurrent engineering involving product engineers; research technologists; quality, reliability, and manufacturing engineers; operations; marketing; customer services; *supply managers; and selected suppliers* are keys to timely introduction of quality products.

Next, we direct our attention to selection of the optimal source.

NOTES

1. For more information on Atlas Door, see Stalk, pp. 38–44.
2. For more on this issue, the interested reader may desire to read "Purchasing's Role in New Product Development," by David N. Burt and William Soukup, *Harvard Business Review* (July–August 1984).
3. Andrea Bonaccorsi, "A Framework for Integrating Technology and Procurement Strategy," *Proceedings of the 8th IMP Conference,* Lyon, France (September 3–5, 1992), p. 34.
4. John A. Carlisle and Robert C. Parker, *Beyond Negotiation: Redeeming Customer-Supplier Relationships* (Chichester, U.K.: John Wiley & Sons, 1989), p. 127.
5. Amy Harmon, "Teamwork: Chrysler Builds a Concept as Well as a Car," *Los Angeles Times* (April 26, 1992), pp. D1–D3.
6. Roger L. Hale *et al., Made in the USA,* p. 69.
7. Interview with Regis McKenna by Anne R. Field, "First Strike," *Success* (October, 1989), p. 48.
8. Adapted from David N. Burt, *Proactive Procurement: The Key to Increased Profits, Productivity, and Quality* (Englewood Cliffs, NJ: Prentice-Hall, Inc., 1984), pp. 25, 27, and 29.

9. "Why G.E. Makes as Little as Possible," *Electronics Purchasing* (March 1992), pp. 25–27.
10. Keki R. Bhote, *World Class Quality*, AMA Management Briefing (New York: American Management Association, 1988).
11. *21st Century Manufacturing Enterprise Strategy*, p. 8.
12. Nobuto, Remarks.

CHAPTER 6

SELECTING AMERICAN
KEIRETSU-TYPE SUPPLIERS

From a strategic point of view, it is desirable to purchase from suppliers who will maintain or improve their competitive position in terms of their products and service.[1]

Michael E. Porter

To produce the best products and services, a firm needs more than great ideas and innovative designs. The firm must also select the best possible suppliers.

Strategic sourcing requires that the manufacturer first determine if the required material or subassembly affects a core competency, strategic technology, and/or competitive position. If it does, a decision must be made whether to make or buy the item—with the buy decision ideally satisfied through a carefully crafted American Keiretsu-type (AKT) relationship.

Bettis, Bradley, and Hamel have conducted extensive research on this issue in North America, Europe, and Asia. They write,

What is important is to view sourcing in strategic and offensive terms instead of merely as a defensive technique for trying to fix problems. . . . This approach to outsourcing decisions requires that they be treated as components of overall strategy, not as incremental decisions. As such, outsourcing should be included in the normal strategy review process and measured in strategic and financial terms.[2]

Selecting a potential AKT supplier from among existing or new suppliers requires the cooperation of many members of the cross-functional Supply Management team. The progression to AKT relationships must be carefully planned and executed. The key ingredients that must be present are strategic fit and mutual trust.

The supply environment is dynamic: rapid advances in technology, product innovations, and tactical and strategic changes by suppliers and competitors in the global market combine to require World-Class firms to monitor their supply environments for both threats and opportunities. Joichi Aoi, president and CEO of Toshiba Corporation, indicates that in Japan the keiretsu structures "differ from industry to industry and vary from year to year, and the relations among constituents are flexible and constantly changing."[3]

TO MAKE OR TO BUY

Frequently, there is no easy or clear-cut answer to the challenging question, "Should we make this product or service or outsource (buy) it?" Several years ago, a president of the Ford Motor Company commented, "At Ford we wasted millions making items we should have bought and buying items we should have made. But we could never figure it out *before* the fact."

In the early 1980s, General Motors, Ford, and Chrysler were all confronted with make-or-buy decisions for their semiconductors. Interestingly enough, one chose a pure buy, one chose to invest heavily in manufacturing capacity, and one chose a hybrid approach without a manufacturing investment. In retrospect, it would appear that each decision was correct based on the unique circumstances at each company. Interestingly, with 10 years of hindsight, it appears that all three strategies have been successful.

Historically, the make/buy decision often has been treated as a tactical issue. Events of the last 10 years involving technology transfer, core competency erosion, and the loss of America's manufacturing base clearly demonstrate that this is a high-order strategic issue requiring a much more thorough review than was common. In most cases, this strategic evaluation can be greatly facilitated through operating procedures that develop and pool all relevant information. The following may be of assistance:

- Core technologies and competencies, both current and future, *must be identified and **must be** protected.*[a] This can be done both through make decisions and through very carefully crafted and managed AKT agreements.

- "Make" decisions may stretch management too thin or increase organizational complexity beyond acceptable limits. (Remember Peters and Waterman's admonishment to "stick to your knitting.")[5]

- "Make" decisions are often more expensive than buy decisions and are frequently hard to reverse. For example, "the enormous investment GM had sunk into its parts operations made it very hard to think about alternatives."[6]

- Internal financial analyses based on traditional cost accounting overhead allocations tend to support a continuation of making—often in spite of overwhelming evidence to the contrary.

- Tradition, established organizational patterns, or purely emotional reasoning often play a major role resulting in both decisions.

Prahalad and Hamel argue that "managers deciding whether to make or buy will start with end products and look upstream to the efficiencies of the supply chain and

---

[a]Prahalad and Hamel write that "at least three tests can be applied to identify core competencies in a company. First, a core competence provides potential access to a wide variety of markets. . . . Second, a core competence should make a significant contribution to the perceived customer benefits of the end product. . . . Finally, a core competence should be difficult for competitors to imitate. . . . *Core competencies are the wellspring of new business development.* (emphasis added); pp. 83–84 and 91.[4]

downstream toward distribution and customers."[7] Charles Ferguson of MIT adds, "Without imminent changes, U.S. and European vendors of information systems hardware risk becoming subordinate research, prototyping, and distribution arms for the Japanese industry's vertically integrated industrial complexes. Most observers agree that subordination would be catastrophic."[8] Welch and Nayak observe:

> When sourcing decisions are examined, managers must ask themselves whether it will be detrimental to their firm's competitive position to outsource R&D, design, engineering, manufacturing, or assembly, both in the short term and in the long term. Managers must determine the importance of process technology in attaining and/or sustaining competitive advantage. Managers must also consider a forecast of those technologies that have the potential to provide significant competitive advantage in the future.[9]

SELECTING SUPPLIERS

In the past, the selection of suppliers was too often the responsibility of well-intentioned engineers and others who were not sensitive to strategic or commercial implications of their decisions or equally well-intentioned buyers with little sensitivity to important technical, quality, and service considerations. Engineers tended to seek suppliers with technologies that advanced the state-of-the-art and improved the performance features of their products. Unsophisticated services customers were more concerned with personal relationships and frequently were easy prey for a skillful marketer. Buyers tended to favor local suppliers and large inventories. The buyers commonly relied on market forces to produce suppliers with the required technological depth, quality, and economic competitiveness.

Experience demonstrates again and again that the selection of suppliers must be a *team* effort. Companies need to have knowledgeable professionals from various departments and functions involved in supplier selection. When sourcing a critical component to a new supplier, progressive companies develop a team typically drawn from Purchasing, design engineering, marketing, operations, manufacturing and quality, finance, and related functions. A modified worksheet similar to that shown in Figure 5-4 may be helpful in identifying appropriate membership. The team must develop specific measurement criteria for the critical purchase requirement and carefully review the potential supplier's capabilities against the criteria in the following representative areas:

- *Management.* History, stability, record of innovation, focus, goals, objectives, and direction.
- *Engineering.* Engineering staff and equipment.
- *Production and Quality.* Production and quality control systems, specific performance records, production and quality processes and disciplines, and applicable measures.
- *Equipment and Facilities.* Appropriate equipment and sufficient capacity.
- *Technology.* R&D, patent position, and CAD/CAM/interface capabilities.
- *Purchasing.* Adequate, effective, and efficient sources of required raw materials and purchased components, disciplined process, and quality capabilities.
- *Financial Resources.* Current financial position, profit record, and net worth.
- *Past Performance.* Reputation, experience, major customers, and appropriate references.

Product development teams should invite selected suppliers to contribute to the design of new parts and to statements of work for service requirements. (When an AKT relationship exists, normally only this supplier will be involved as new items and services are typically pre-sourced.) For an algorithm on this complicated decision, see Figure 6–1. The supply team analyzes supplier suggestions and contributions in the areas of design, quality plans, work plans, and cost projections.

The Benefits and Risks of Foreign Sourcing

International sourcing requires additional efforts when compared with domestic sourcing, but it can yield large rewards. A recent *Harvard Business Review* article reported on the success of partnerships of 150 top companies ranked by market value. Fifty of the firms were from the United States, 50 from Japan, and 50 from Europe. Forty-nine strategic alliances for the development and/or marketing of products were studied in detail. The analysis revealed "that although cross-border alliances pose many challenges, they are in fact viable vehicles for international strategy."[10] For example, 15 percent of the value of Toshiba laptop computers is purchased from non-Japanese sources. Foreign suppliers can make excellent supply partners *if, and only if, the buying firm protects its core technologies.* One of the complexities of buying goods and services of foreign origin is the wide variability among the producing countries in characteristics such as quality, service, and dependability. With this caveat in mind, common reasons for purchasing foreign goods and services are now introduced.

Quality. Discussions with American executives lead to a surprising conclusion: the number-one reason for foreign sourcing is to obtain the required level of quality. In coming years, this factor is bound to decline in significance as American suppliers continue to address their quality problems and adopt the total quality commitment concept. Unfortunately, at the moment many buyers in a variety of industries still look offshore to fulfill their most critical quality requirements.

FIGURE 6–1
Strategic Sourcing Decision Algorithm

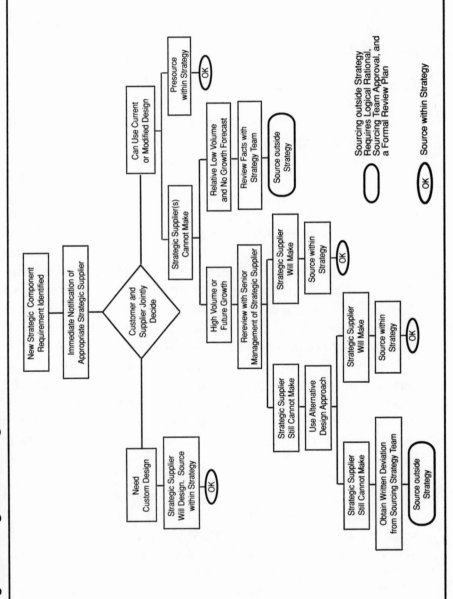

Timeliness.   A second major reason given by professionals involved in the purchase of foreign goods and services is the dependability of the supplier in meeting schedule requirements. Once initial difficulties of the new business relationship have been overcome, many foreign sources have proven to be remarkably dependable. In this area, too, the performance of American suppliers has improved markedly during the last several years and, in all likelihood, will continue to become more reliable and more service-oriented. The growing use of flexible manufacturing systems and the increasing use of tightly controlled production planning systems enables some American firms to equal or exceed the performance of their foreign competitors. AKT relationships will accelerate this trend.

Cost.   International sourcing generates expenses beyond those normally encountered when sourcing domestically. For example, additional communications and transportation expenses, import duties, and greater costs when investigating the potential supplier's capabilities add to the buyer's total costs. To illustrate the point, one major computer manufacturer uses a rule of thumb that a foreign material's price must be at least 20 percent lower than the comparable domestic price to compensate for these additional costs. *Nonetheless,* after all of the additional costs of "buying foreign" are considered, in the case of many materials, it is frequently possible to reduce the firm's *total cost* through international sourcing.

New Technologies.   No country holds a monopoly on innovation or advances in technology. Foreign sources in some industries tend to be more advanced technologically than their American counterparts. Not to take advantage of such advanced technology can result in a manufacturer's losing its competitive position vis-a-vis manufacturers that incorporate the new technology.

Finding World Class Suppliers.   World Class manufacturers must develop and maintain a World Class supply base for required materials in order to maintain their leadership position. It may be necessary for domestic firms to develop foreign suppliers in order to compete on a global basis. Product and process technology concerns must be addressed. Many countries require nondomestic suppliers to purchase materials and services in their country as part of the sales transaction. These arrangements are commonly called barter, offsets, or countertrade. The tying of sales into a country with the purchase of goods and services from that country increases the complexity for both the marketing department and Purchasing. These countertrade transactions are far more challenging than pure monetary transactions. For a buyer's firm to compete and make sales in many countries, increasingly it is necessary to enter into agreements to purchase items made in those countries. This is another important consideration which impacts the growing strategic importance of the firm's Supply Management function.[b]

Problems Associated with Foreign Procurement

The Big Danger
In a broad sense, *the biggest danger in buying goods and services of foreign origin is the long-term impact on the U.S. standard of living.* Stephen Cohen and John Zysman in their provocative book, *Manufacturing Matters,* argue that the ability of the American economy to maintain high and rising wages under conditions of openness to international competition is *not* enhanced by abandoning production to others.[12] Akio Morita, the chairman of Sony, warns America: "Unless U.S. industry shores up its manufacturing base, it could lose everything. American companies have either shifted output to low-wage countries or come to buy parts and assembled products from countries like Japan that can make quality

---

[b]For an in-depth review, see *Creative Countertrade* by Kenton W. Elderkin and Warren E. Norquist.[11]

products at low prices. The result is a hollowing of American industry. The United States is abandoning its status as an industrial power."[13]

Selected American firms, including many divisions of General Electric Co., IBM, and Hewlett-Packard, in addition to Honda of America, Millken and Company, Harley-Davidson, and America President Lines, Ltd., work with their domestic suppliers to develop them into World Class manufacturers that compete successfully with nondomestic suppliers. Thus, the buying firm, the supplier, and the American economy all benefit. These domestic supplier arrangements are established and structured based on formal research and analysis and supplier development. Strategic evaluation, sourcing and coordination, and open negotiations are replacing the ineffective Procurement Processes of the past. This requires a major new paradigm: Supply Management. *The Procurement Processes American industry has used for so long are obsolete and no longer apply!*

SELECTING PARTNERS

Progression to AKT agreements doesn't just happen. These agreements are the result of considerable study and analysis to ensure that the suppliers are the most desirable available. The key ingredients for any successful AKT relationship are strategic fit and trust. Obviously, a potential supplier must demonstrate (or be willing and able to develop) the required engineering, quality, capacity, responsiveness, flexibility, cost, and dependability. But if it is not possible after a reasonable period of time to develop an open, trusting relationship, then this is *not* the right supplier. *The issue here is the serious commitment to push continuous improvement jointly throughout the value chain.*

SINGLE VERSUS DUAL SOURCING

Questions concerning single and dual sourcing are frequently raised. American managers appear to be about evenly split on this issue. Some express grave concerns about "putting all their eggs into one basket"; others have come to believe that single sourcing is the best choice for their firm.

> Often, a single vendor simply has not had the capacity to meet the customer's demand. Rather than encourage and even help a single vendor to acquire the required capacity, it has been easier for manufacturers to buy from multiple suppliers simultaneously. Conversely, many suppliers have been reluctant to supply 100 percent of a customer's requirements, even when they have sufficient capacity or could invest in more.[14]

Howard and Shelly Gitlow in their book *The Deming Guide to Quality and Competitive Position* argue that "instead of spending a great deal of effort disaster-proofing a firm by creating a large supply base for each purchased item, management should search for a single supplier for each item who exhibits financial stability, labor stability, quality-conscious management, political stability, statistical process control, low or no downtime, dependable vendor relations, etc."[15] In other words, find one supplier who meets 100 percent of all of the requirements before expending time and energy locating a second source.

This single/dual decision is much more complex than one would initially expect. There are numerous critical trade-offs to be considered. *Each sourcing decision contains its own dynamics which defy simple analysis and sweeping generalizations.* The question "Should a firm typically single source or typically dual source its purchased components?" has no answer and may even be the wrong question. Over time many firms have developed informal departmental practices that direct buyer action on this question one way or the other. These practices are generally dysfunctional, as their effect often reduces analysis and substitutes rote process for critical analysis.

It is interesting to note that dual sourcing is quite common in Japan unless excessive investments are required for the second source. Some Japanese manufacturers use this approach to motivate the supplier receiving the larger share of the customer's business to provide the required levels of quality and service.

> When a supplier falls short on quality or reliability, the assembler does not dismiss the company—the normal method in the West. Instead, the assembler shifts a fraction of the business from that supplier to its other source for that part for a given period of time as a penalty.[16]

More commonly, Japanese manufacturers define *dual sourcing* as a process of establishing two suppliers with the capability and resources (e.g., tooling) required to provide quality materials. However, the customer firm receives materials from only one of these suppliers in order to reduce variability. The investment in the redundant tooling at the back-up supplier is made to minimize the risk of supply disruptions.

In an effort to provide the reader with an overview of the complexity involved in this apparently simple issue, many (but certainly not all) of the considerations requiring analysis are listed in Figure 6-2.

CONCLUDING REMARKS

Source selection is a strategic activity and must be a cross-functional activity. The team must determine the firm's areas of core competencies when deciding to make or to buy the required material. If the decision is to buy, the team must carefully review available potential suppliers and choose one that is, or has the potential of becoming, World Class. But

FIGURE 6–2
The Single/Dual Sourcing Dilemma

Perceived Strengths of Single Sourcing

- Improved quality—less supplier induced variation.
- Improved supplier commitment.
- Possible reductions of the supply base.
- Improved joint interdependency/risk sharing.
- Less complex communication network.
- Improved facilitation of technology sharing.
- Possible improvement in velocity (time to market and cycle time).
- Reduction in total system inventory.
- Improved economies of scale (manufacturing, packaging, freight, program management, invoicing, etc.).

Perceived Strengths of Dual Sourcing

- Volume—capacity requirement.
- Requirement during supplier development phase.
- Possible requirement for selected off-shore sourcing.
- Requirement for certain components, markets, and suppliers.
- Possible requirement for strike protection.
- Convenience for standard or distributor type items.
- Facilitation of selected minority or small business sourcing programs.
- Facilitation of selected local content requirements.
- Facilitation of selected global marketing initiatives.
- Continuity—long-term sourcing history with two outstanding suppliers of the same commodity or commodity class.

selecting such a supplier is not enough. The supplier must be motivated to remain World Class and performance must be monitored, measured, and reported.

We now shift our attention to the management and control of cost within the value chain.

NOTES

1. Michael E. Porter, *Competitive Strategy: Techniques for Analyzing Industries and Competitors* (The Free Press, 1980), p. 123.
2. Richard A. Bettis, Stephen P. Bradley, and Gary Hamel, "Outsourcing and Industrial Decline," *Academy of Management Executive*, 6, no. 1 (1992), p. 18.
3. Joichi Aoi, "Can a Keiretsu Work in America?" Letter to the Editor, *Harvard Business Review* (September–October, 1990), p. 181.
4. For an in-depth discussion of this important topic, see C. K. Prahalad and Gary Hamel, "The Core Competence of the Corporation," *Harvard Business Review* (May–June, 1990), pp. 79–91.
5. Thomas J. Peters and Robert H. Waterman, "Stick to Your Knitting," *In Search of Excellence* (New York: Harper & Row, 1982), pp. 292–305.
6. James P. Womack, Daniel T. Jones, and Daniel Roos, *The Machine That Changed the World* (New York: Harper Perennial, 1991), p. 139.
7. Prahalad and Hamel, "The Core Competence, p. 83.
8. Charles H. Ferguson, "Computers and the Coming of the U.S. Keiretsu," *Harvard Business Review* (July–August 1990), p. 66.
9. James A. Welch and P. Ranganath Nayak, "Strategic Sourcing: A Progressive Approach to the Make-or-Buy Decision," *Academy of Management Executive* 6, no. 1 (1992), p. 23.
10. Joel Bleeke and David Ernst, "The Way to Win in Cross-Border Alliances," *Harvard Business Review* (November–December 1991), p. 127.
11. Kenton W. Elderkin and Warren E. Norquist, *Creative Countertrade* (Cambridge, MA: Ballinger Publishing Company, 1987).
12. Stephen Cohen and John Zysman, *Manufacturing Matters* (New York: Basic Books, Inc., 1987).
13. *Ibid.*, p. 60.
14. Roy L. Harmon and Leroy D. Peterson, "Reinventing the Factory," *Productivity Breakthroughs in Manufacturing Today* (New York: Free Press, 1990), p. 258.
15. Howard S. Gitlow and Shelly J. Gitlow, *The Deming Guide to Quality and Competitive Position* (Englewood Cliffs, NJ: Prentice-Hall, Inc., 1987), pp. 56–57.
16. Womack et al, *The Machine* p. 154.

CHAPTER 7

VALUE-CHAIN COST MANAGEMENT

Those who can make a product cheaper can take it away from the inventor. In today's world it does very little good to invent a new product if the inventor is not the cheapest producer of that product.[1]

Lester Thurow

Chapter 1 introduced the principle that competition is conducted between value chains focused on the ultimate consumer. *One of Supply Management's greatest challenges is to maximize value and minimize costs throughout the upstream portion of the value chain.* This challenge requires that manufacturers and firms in process and service industries, their suppliers, and their suppliers' suppliers *must* focus their collective efforts on reducing the total cost of materials, services, and processes used within their value chain. Such a focus requires knowledge and sensitivity throughout the value chain to identify cost elements and work to reduce the total cost associated with the Procurement Process and the conversion of materials. The formation and management of American Keiretsu-type (AKT) alliances is the most effective and efficient legal way for American firms to maximize value throughout the value chain.

As relative value, product and quality leverage, and cost increase, price becomes a less important consideration among many variables. Agreement on these many issues must be reached through open and collaborative negotiations.

Frequently the role of profit is not understood by young or inexperienced Purchasing personnel. Profit must correlate with the amount of risk involved in the product, technology, and so forth. A reasonable profit is necessary to ensure that AKT suppliers remain in business and attract sufficient investments to support competitive levels of R&D spending, plant and equipment modernization, and training. Some large, well-known firms continue to overemploy their economic leverage to negotiate lower and lower prices for their own short-term advantage. In the longer term, they are planting the seeds for future competitive disaster as they erode their supply base and ultimately their global competitiveness. *This traditional short-sighted, price-focused approach to industrial procurement is one of the major contributors to the economic and competitive difficulties currently facing America. The answer, in the majority of cases, is enlightened Supply Management, not vertical integration.*

STRATEGIC COST MANAGEMENT

Strategic cost management provides a conceptual framework that supports the firm's efforts to reduce costs within the value chain. John Shank, in his 1989 article "Strategic Cost Management: New Wine, or Just New Bottles?" defines strategic cost management as the managerial use of cost information *explicitly* divested at one or more of the four stages of the strategic management cycle:

- Formulating (and integrating) strategies.
- Communicating those strategies throughout the organization.
- Developing and carrying out tactics to implement the strategies.
- Developing and implementing controls to monitor the

success of the implementation steps and hence success in meeting the strategic objectives.

Strategic cost management blends three underlying themes:

- Value chain analysis.
- Strategic positioning analysis.
- Cost driver analysis.[2]

Shank's focus on these three analyses is of particular interest and parallels many of the principles advanced in this book. His "value-chain analysis" recognizes that actions taken to reduce costs in the buying firm may be more than offset by additional costs created with the firm's upstream suppliers. "Value chain analysis" also complements actions taken during product design (Chapter 5) to minimize the customer's costs associated with the use of the end product.

"Strategic positioning analysis" supports the firm's need to understand the costs associated with purchasing and converting purchased materials and then field costs resulting from consumption of the end product.

"Cost driver analysis" requires understanding the complex interplay of the set of drivers at work in any given situation. Two of these drivers (scale and scope) affect sourcing decisions through the make-or-buy analysis discussed in Chapter 6.

TOTAL COST

Based on personal observations and interviews with dozens of executives in many industries, it is apparent that most buyers are "price" oriented. This results largely from management evaluating buyers on their ability to get the lowest price. Often, a purchase price variance report is the only formal measure of purchasing performance. Unfortunately, the lowest price frequently does not result in the lowest "all-in-cost" or total cost from the perspective of the firm's total cost of operations. Measures like purchase price variance tend to drive dysfunctional behavior among buyers.

Chapter 1 introduced the charge that organizations must change their focus from purchase price to consideration of the total cost involved in purchasing, transporting, storing, handling, and converting material and using services. This total cost includes purchase price, incoming transportation, and the following in-house costs: storage, handling, waste in the area of lost productivity, process yield losses, scrap and re-work resulting from suboptimal purchased materials. Warranty and field service costs, customer returns, and the cost of lost sales attributable in whole or in part to customer dissatisfaction with products incorporating defective purchased materials are included in the definition of total costs. The components of total purchased material cost were portrayed in Chapter 1, which is repeated here as Figure 7-1 for the reader's convenience.

FIGURE 7-1
The Total Cost of Materials and Services

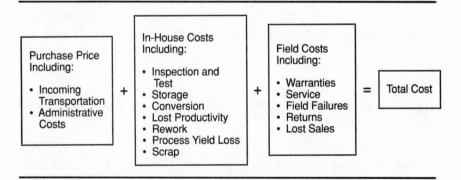

Source: Adapted from David N. Burt, Warren E. Norquist, and Jimmy Anklesaria, *Zero Base Pricing*™: *Achieving World Class Competitiveness through Reduced All-In-Costs* (Chicago, Ill.: Probus Publishing Company, 1990).

Need for an Improved Management Information System

It is most unfortunate that purchase price is so relatively easy to identify while in-house costs, incoming transportation, and field failure costs are so much more difficult to identity— even to estimate. While the identification of these costs may be difficult, it does not mean that they do not exist or need not be managed aggressively! Hopefully, the managerial accounting function will aggressively adopt the principles of activity-based costing. *Implementation of these modern cost-accounting techniques is on the critical path leading to global competitiveness.*

In order to make sound business decisions, buyers must understand quantitatively the difference in costs between incoming material with a likely defect rate of 50 parts per million versus incoming material with a likely defect rate of 500 parts per million. With this information, the Supply Management team may estimate the likely total cost of the two materials of differing quality levels and make more cost-effective decisions. When obtaining services from a supplier who always completes work on time and one who has a history of delinquency, the Supply Management team must understand the cost implication of these two levels of service. Without total cost data, decisions are often made based on price quotations alone. This is an ineffective method that produces random results.

TOTAL COST MANAGEMENT BEGINS AT THE DESIGN STAGE

It is estimated that 70 to 85 percent of avoidable total costs are controllable at the design stage. Early involvement of carefully selected suppliers and adherence to the practices introduced throughout this book are essential activities in the firm's efforts to reduce total cost. Increasingly, firms are employing the design of experiments (DOE) in an effort to design variability and cost out of their products and out of their purchased materials, components, subassemblies, and services. Through the use of DOE techniques, it is possible to identify the critical variables or parameters that affect quality and costs of the item under design. *The result is a robust design—one which will be virtually defect free at reduced cost.* A second benefit resulting from the use of DOE is that noncritical variables are also identified. The tolerances for these variables can be relaxed, frequently resulting in significantly lower costs. Once these activities have been accomplished, a reasonable purchase price that is fair to both organizations can be negotiated. The agreement must include continuous improvement objectives in both quality and cost.

PRICE AND COST ANALYSIS[a]

Historically, competitive bidding has been the mainspring of clever pricing strategies. The use of competitive bidding may be acceptable with low-value, noncritical procurements. But the use of negotiation is more appropriate when establishing pricing for relatively higher-value requirements, with one important proviso: price and, where possible, cost analysis must be conducted to ensure that the value chain is and remains competitive.

Negotiations are the optimal way of ensuring clarity between the two parties and establishing sound agreements. *By understanding the cost structure, the buyer can ensure that outstanding value is being received and that costs do not drop to a level where quality and/or service may be compromised.*

Under AKT relationships, both parties must work together to squeeze cost out of the value chain, including inter-

---

[a]For a much more detailed review of price and cost analysis, briefly overviewed here, see Burt, Norquist, and Anklesaria, *Zero Base Pricing*™.

organizational costs. The supplier should be motivated through the long-term relationship to identify and submit value analysis proposals. For example, specifications, tolerances, and related requirements must be examined jointly in an effort to meet the ultimate customer's needs at the lowest possible cost.

Price Analysis

Price analysis is the evaluation and review of the total price of an item without regard to the individual elements of cost or profit. It focuses on the bottom-line price. This is a relatively simple and inexpensive method of determining that the price is reasonable or that selected prices track published industry trends.

Price analysis is based on a process of comparison. The buyer compares the supplier's price trend with other potential suppliers' proposals, historic costs adjusted to offset inflation, industry price index data, commodity index data, and/or engineered estimates. As the supply relationship progresses to AKT relationship status, competitive prices will be unavailable. Cost estimates developed by the buying firm's estimating department, or jointly developed with the supplier, must become the principle basis of comparison. When price analysis does not support a conclusion that a price is fair and reasonable, or when employing the design-to-cost approach to pricing described later in this chapter, cost analysis must be employed.

Cost Analysis

Cost analysis requires an examination of every cost element including direct and indirect costs and profit. (See Figure 7–2.)

As part of the evolution to AKT relationships, the supplier must, at an appropriate point, share cost data with the

FIGURE 7–2
Suppliers' Cost and Profit Model

Profit
General and Administrative
Overhead
Direct Labor
Direct Materials

Source: Adapted from David N. Burt, Warren E. Norquist, and Jimmy Anklesaria, *Zero Base Pricing*™: *Achieving World Class Competitiveness through Reduced All-In-Costs* (Chicago, Ill.: Probus Publishing Company, 1990).

customer firm. In some cases, it may be necessary to develop a cost model, or to use detailed estimates developed by the cost-estimating organization to assist the cost analyst in understanding the supplier's likely costs. The cost analyst's job is to identify costs requiring further investigation. Negotiations over direct costs are normally far less challenging than those dealing with indirect costs. Standard cost systems and overhead allocation schemes vary widely between firms. These cost systems require careful review and attention if AKT suppliers are to cooperate in maximizing value and the success of their value chain.

Normally, agreement is possible on both direct and indirect costs. It is noted that firms are increasingly implementing activity based costing (ABC). This work assists management in two critical areas: (1) it allows the firm to make better estimates of in-house and field failure costs; (2) ABC simplifies Supply Management's task of agreeing with the supplier what realistic overheads should be charged to the material or service being supplied.

With an Activity Based Costing (ABC) system:

- Labor is combined with overhead into conversion cost.
- All manufacturing costs are assigned to products.
- Simplistic overhead allocation methods are scrapped.
- *Many* allocation bases are used instead of a single base.
- ABC focuses on who controls costs: engineers, planners, schedulers, maintenance, and so forth.
- Equipment is "rented" by production departments at market prices.
- Standard costs are used less for control purposes. Actual costs are monitored more closely.
- ABC moves toward job costing.
- ABC recognizes that 70 to 85 percent of costs for new products/processes will be committed before production.
- Recognizing the shortening of product life cycles, ABC allows quicker recovery of product development costs.[b]

When there is an irreconcilable difference on direct and/or indirect costs, the following modern procurement techniques may help the parties reach an equitable agreement.

---

[b]For more insight into activity based costing, the interested reader is referred to the Spring 1990 issue of the *Journal of Cost Management*, which is devoted to this issue; Robert S. Kaplan's article, "One Cost System Isn't Enough" (*Harvard Business Review*, January–February 1988); and Robin Cooper and Robert S. Kaplan's article, "Measure Costs Right: Make the Right Decisions" (*Harvard Business Review*, September–October, 1988).

Should Cost.   On occasion, it may be necessary for the buying firm to develop a team of manufacturing, industrial, and quality engineers; Purchasing; and financial experts to review the supplier's operation. This is a cooperative action conducted with the supplier's agreement and full involvement. This team identifies areas requiring specific upgrades while simultaneously developing (with the supplier's personnel participating) the amount the item *should cost* when produced under the resulting upgraded processes.

An American-based Japanese manufacturer invested over two man-years of such assistance with one of its American suppliers. This supplier now meets this customer's competitive cost objectives and has improved its market share within its industry.

Incentive Contracts.   On occasion, the amount of risk and uncertainty present in a project may make the use of the conventional firm fixed price method of compensation inappropriate. There is an array of pricing mechanisms specifically designed to motivate suppliers to meet the competitive needs of an important project in a cost-efficient manner.

Profit

Unfortunately, profit is not properly employed in the majority of procurements. Profit must attract good suppliers and stimulate effective and efficient performance. Harmon and Peterson write,

> Superior manufacturers will realize that successful suppliers must earn a reasonable return on their investment in order to be, and to remain, superior suppliers. Two compelling reasons support this conclusion:
> 1. No reasonable management or board of directors would permit a business to continuously operate with marginal profits, or even losses. The supplier that is forced to sell at prices too low to bring a reasonable return on investment

must move into other product lines or customers and/or abandon unprofitable business.

2. Process and product designs must be continuously improved. This requires investment in research and development, and in capital expenditures. Suppliers cannot invest in these areas, however, unless profits are adequate. Further, if the supplier perceives a high likelihood of losing a customer's business at some point, he would, naturally, favor investment in other areas of higher return and greater security.[3]

Profit must:

- Reward suppliers for the risks they assume.
- Motivate suppliers to undertake challenging work.
- Motivate suppliers to increase their efficiency.
- Reward highly dependable suppliers.
- Reward suppliers employing highly skilled personnel.
- Reward suppliers who deliver exceptionally reliable technical products.
- Encourage desirable suppliers to take a long-term view.
- Provide sufficient reward to ensure that the supplier remains technologically advanced and has competitive access to capital.

Design-to-Cost

The American automotive and some elements of the defense industry have long used a design-to-cost approach to pricing of numerous assemblies and subassemblies. As observed in Chapter 2, this is a common method of pricing in Japan. With design-to-cost (DTC), the manufacturer estimates the selling price the market will bear for the desired number of units of production of the end item (e.g., car, toaster, or industrial robot). This is converted to a target cost to manufacture or assemble. As appropriate, this target cost to produce is, in turn, allocated to the principle subsystems on down to the component level. Costs are allocated out at each stage of production. The buyer and seller of purchased assemblies, subassemblies, and commodities then negotiate—not on price, but rather on how to reach the target price while allowing a reasonable profit objective for the supplier.

One of the interesting adaptations of DTC is the incorporation of a programmed rate of learning or cost improvement. The aerospace, defense, and construction industry have used learning-curve methodology to good advantage. Continuous improvement requirements for cost are used in the Japanese auto industry and are increasingly common in the American auto industry. Their use requires management, design and process engineering, operations, and Purchasing to apply their best efforts to drive cost out of the process!

CHANGED CONDITIONS

One of the most challenging aspects of cost management results from changed conditions. Such changes may impact directly on either party. Changing economic and competitive conditions may force the customer to examine all avenues available to lower product costs. Material costs are a particularly attractive target for cost reductions since these are normally the largest single-cost element. Often, material costs are two to five times that of direct labor. In a similar manner, forces beyond a supplier's control may impact on its production costs and open discussions on price increases.

When changed economic conditions make a product less profitable, the parties must review the specific data for the product. Experience indicates that when firms enjoy mutually beneficial relationships, they take considerable interest in cost and profit pressures throughout the value chain. These AKT partners may be able to offer valuable insight and suggestions for improvement. Quite obviously, keeping their product's value chain viable will be in the combined best interests of the parties to the AKT relationship.

Conversely, when changed economic conditions adversely affect a key supplier, the buying firm should be willing to discuss and investigate the changed conditions. Before granting relief, the firm must investigate the actual impact of the changed conditions. During the early 1980s, our colleague, Warren Norquist (vice president, International Purchasing and Materials Management, Polaroid), observed many suppliers who claimed that inflation had destroyed their profitability. By examining the suppliers' actual costs, Mr. Norquist and his buyers were able to reduce the price paid on many items—even in the face of inflation rates of 18 to 20 percent!

The key concept to be employed when either party is severely impacted by changed economic conditions should be: *What is best for the value chain and what is best for the ultimate consumer?*

CONTINUOUS IMPROVEMENT

To this point, the focus of this chapter has been the establishment of the initial purchase price. But this should only be the starting point! Price- and cost-reduction objectives during production must be established if the parties desire to remain globally competitive. Action plans should be developed and implemented. Progress in cost reduction and quality improvement must be measured, and necessary corrective actions should be taken, as appropriate, within the value chain.

CONCLUDING REMARKS

The total cost of materials, not purchase price, must be the focus of parties to AKT relationships. The formation and subsequent management of AKT alliances is the most effective and efficient legal way for American firms to maximize value throughout the value chain. The joint efforts of the partners will squeeze waste out of the system, resulting in a cost-competitive value chain.

The next chapter addresses the AKT procurement of nonproduction and service requirements.

NOTES

1. Lester Thurow, *Head to Head* (New York: Alfred Morrow and Company, 1992), p. 47.
2. John K. Shank, "Strategic Cost Management: New Wine, or Just New Bottles?" *Journal of Management Accounting Research* (Fall 1989), p. 50.
3. Roy L. Harmon and Leroy D. Peterson, "Reinventing the Factory," *Productivity Breakthroughs in Manufacturing Today* (New York: Free Press, 1990), p. 258.

CHAPTER 8

NONPRODUCTION AND SERVICE REQUIREMENTS

The force of core competence is felt as decisively in services as in manufacturing.[1]

C. K. Prahalad and Gary Hamel

The procurement of nonproduction materials and service requirements is a frequently overlooked area for improvement. While the cost implications alone may *suggest* significant attention, the productivity implications *demand* it! Process manufacturing plants, assembly plants, and pipeline operators are idled for want of a bearing, valve, or pump. Banks and other financial institutions cease to operate when their computers or even heating/cooling systems are "down." Productivity and internal efficiency can be greatly affected by these purchased inputs.

With only minor common-sense adaptations, American Keiretsu concepts and techniques can be applied profitably to all the diverse spending requirements of any firm. At the process level, there is very little difference between acquiring a strategic direct material, contracting for corporate legal services, or purchasing motors, bearings, or belts for the maintenance department. Brief applications of these techniques to selected nonproduction and service requirements of common interest are described in this chapter. This discussion is provided as a representative sample of the many possibilities for investigation, analysis, and formal improvement initiative.

CAPITAL EQUIPMENT

Capital equipment also offers important opportunities for strategic Supply Management and American Keiretsu-type (AKT) relationships. Each capital purchase event is unique and, therefore, requires individual analysis and a customized approach.

Chapter 5 addressed the importance of timely procurement of required production and test equipment. The life cycle cost approach to selecting and pricing allows the purchaser to determine the most likely cost of owning and operating an item over its anticipated productive life. This is the only rational approach to determining a true basis for comparing the costs of owning and operating equipment. Further, by considering all the significant costs over the life of the item instead of merely the initial acquisition cost, the firm may gain from increased competition. Firms whose products have higher initial prices but lower subsequent ownership costs may be able to compete and well may offer maximum value.

The cost of ownership incorporates such items as:

- Initial cost of the item together with installation and start-up costs.
- Operating costs (fuel or power consumption, operators' salaries, etc.).
- Finance costs.
- Training costs.
- Maintenance costs.
- Insurance costs.
- Tax considerations.
- Salvage value.

The present value of the expected stream of expenditures less the expected salvage value is generally employed to accommodate the time utility of money. A model portraying

FIGURE 8–1
Total Cost of Ownership

$$TCO = A + P.V.\left[\sum_{i=1}^{n} (T_i + O_i + M_i) - S_n \right]$$

TCO = total cost of ownership
A = acquisition cost
P.V. = present value at the company's cost of money
Σ = the sum of the terms in ( ) from years i to n
T_i = training costs in year i
Q_i = operating costs in year i
M_i = maintenance in year i
S_n = salvage value in year n

Note: Many firms employ capital appropriation analysis similar to this and purchase capital using the cost of ownership. Few firms, however, audit the actual performance against their forecast model. This is an important and critical discipline. These finance models require feedback if they are to be relied on to forecast the cost of ownership on future projects accurately.

this concept is contained in Figure 8–1. The model represents a simplified example wherein initial (acquisition) cost, training costs, operating costs, maintenance costs, and salvage value are the only variables under consideration. When comparing two or more pieces of capital equipment, management should use the item's total cost of ownership, *not* the initial acquisition price.

Often, firms have capital purchase requirements that recur year to year. These unique capital requirements offer special opportunities. An analysis of historical trends and future planned requirements can be completed to evaluate potential sourcing opportunities. Without changing its current policies regarding capital budgeting, planning, and authorization requests, the firm can establish a parallel system to handle these repetitive capital expenditures. By evaluating these needs through time and forecasting, requirement trends can be identified. Cross-functional teams can evaluate suppliers and develop long-term optimum sourcing strategies. At this point, these capital requirements could be "sourced" similar to any major direct material requirement with long-term forecasts and shorter-term commitments. *Such action changes the "look" of these procurements from single independent events to multiple combined opportunities with important cost, lead time, and quality improvement implications.*

This changed sourcing approach holds the potential for significant cost and time savings for both the buying firm and for suppliers. Some firms have implemented this capital purchasing alternative for repetitive capital requirements.

MAINTENANCE REQUIREMENTS

This complex and diverse purchase requirement, commonly called MRO (maintenance, repair and operating supplies), offers vast opportunities for improvement. At the same time, this area offers a professional challenge for AKT implementation. Firms in process industries (paper mills, oil production, food processing, etc.), in service industries (transportation, finance, research, etc.), as well as manufacturers, should initiate aggressive, COO-sponsored effectiveness initiatives in this area. These initiatives should be broad-based and focus on the Procurement Process. The profit improvement and productivity potential available to these firms is outstanding and inadequately exploited. It is important to realize that each MRO commodity represents a special situation that requires a customized approach.

Important MRO expenditures are often overshadowed by much higher expenditures for direct materials. At many firms, accounting techniques tend to mask the importance of the MRO expenditures. These supplies are often recorded at standard cost (including freight) and expensed upon receipt. MRO material costs are often combined with maintenance labor and other miscellaneous expenses and reported as one line item. Part usage, price, and sourcing trend data commonly are not maintained, complicating efforts at trend analysis, committal contract buying, inventory stocking programs, coordinated contracting, and so forth.

MRO buyers at many firms simply place orders, process paper, and confirm purchases previously made by the maintenance department or other personnel. The attitude typically encountered is one of resignation: "Maintenance is a complicated process that offers little opportunity for management or control. As long as the maintenance budget is not seriously overrun and the plant continues to operate, things must be OK."

This laissez-faire approach is a serious competitive issue in our global economy. Some companies have taken an aggressive proactive approach to maintenance purchases. Many have learned that when the maintenance activity and the MRO Supply Management process are intertwined, there is considerable opportunity for improvement.

The ultimate process should incorporate an integrated strategy as shown in Figure 8–2—"Maintenance Process Interdependence." This model shows that, as the maintenance process moves from *Reactive* to *Preventative* to *Predictive*, the MRO Procurement Process may progress from *Reactive* to *Proactive* to *Strategic*. Maximum effectiveness can only be achieved when both of these interdependent processes are linked and operating at the predictive (strategic) stage. Although this is the ultimate stage of progression, firms should not delay improving the Procurement Process for the implementation of predictive maintenance. Considerable improvement during the progression to strategic Supply Management can be made in the current MRO Procurement Process at most firms.

As outlined in the February 1992 issue of *Industrial Distribution*, Bethlehem Steel's Burns Harbor plant has viewed MRO as a strategic opportunity. Over the past eight years, this facility has developed system contracts with selected

FIGURE 8–2
Maintenance Process Interdependence

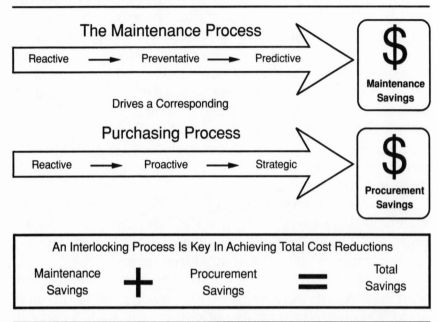

MRO distributors. Burns Harbor has documented benefits
and savings in the areas of (1) reduced man hours, (2) reduced
inventories, (3) lower purchase prices, (4) supplier-identified
cost savings initiatives, and (5) reduced administrative costs.
Over the past eight years, this plant has documented total
savings in excess of $5 million per year. Lower purchase
prices represent only a small portion of these savings, however; nearly half were achieved through the reduction of
man-hours formerly spent searching for parts.

Bearings Example

The following example of the MRO purchasing practices at
a large multinational process industry firm is offered to illustrate the opportunities available in the area of MRO procurement.

The firm uses blanket order releases (BORs) for storeroom purchases. These BORs are not systems contracts: they are spot-buy in nature. BORs are used primarily to improve Purchasing department efficiency. However, they do not contribute to volume purchase leverage potential. Actually, they increase the total paperwork when measured processwide.

Well over half of all storeroom items were covered by BORs at this firm. These items were competitively bid from time to time. There was no policy that outlined the minimum frequency of such bid solicitations. Because past usage data retention was limited and future maintenance requirements were not forecast, quoted items typically were bid with a volume quantity requirement of one. The firm had approximately 100 BORs in place. Due to MRO purchasing workload, these agreements were often rolled over each year with the current supplier, without competitive review.

The MRO Purchasing group had an informal agreement with the accounts payable group to "pay on pass" all invoices for MRO materials containing price increases up to 5 percent. This practice was not documented and was established some years ago in an effort to reduce the volume workload for supplier invoice "kick-outs." The firm did not have measures in place that would show the rollover practice, the 5 percent price increase practice, or the total cost impact of these decisions.

The firm had a large BOR on bearings. The agreement required the supplier to hold inventory locally for supply protection. Bearings were and are a high-volume maintenance item for this firm. In the past 18 months, the firm has used over 4,000 total bearings consisting of over 500 different part numbers, at a cost of approximately $300,000.

	Specific Part Numbers	Volume (total)	Total Cost for 18 months
18 months bearing activity:	500	4,000 (units)	$300,000

Three hundred and seventy-five of these bearings, representing $180,000 of the expenditure, were actually covered on the firm's BOR agreement. The other 125 bearings were purchased on a BOR form but outside of the official BOR system. These bearings were ordered and delivered on the back-up system, "price on request," which covers odd items required from time to time that are not included on the official BOR list of priced part numbers.

Interestingly, the firm maintains considerable inventory both within its storeroom and at the supplier's local warehouse, as shown:

Bearing Inventory	Part Nos.	Quantity	Days' Supply	$ Value
Storeroom	1500	2000	110	$400,000
Supplier	400	1000	55	$450,000
Total:	1900	3000	165	$850,000

The supplier holds higher-cost bearings as directed by Purchasing. This is done to "reduce inventory carrying costs." The supplier holds this inventory specifically for this contract. This practice represents an undocumented contingent liability to the firm.

The supplier's "inventory carrying costs" are simply added to the purchase prices of parts at the time they are delivered. If this added expense is less than 5 percent, the invoice is automatically approved, based on the "pay on pass" process.

The supplier delivers bearings to this firm an average of 10 times per day and maintains a truck and two drivers to support this delivery requirement around the clock. The supplier generates over 2,400 invoices per year. This volume of paper contributes to the lack of analysis. "Finding out what is really going on with bearings is a big job!"

The last time the bearing BOR was competitively bid was 1989. The practice of requesting quotations on a long list of part numbers without consideration of volume information drives extremely dysfunctional results. The current supplier has volume profile history (even if Purchasing doesn't) and, therefore, has the opportunity to rig the bidding. The current supplier simply develops a quotation containing deep discounts on known low-volume part numbers and slightly higher prices on known higher-volume part numbers. This practice results in a lower total piece price when the unit bid prices are added together to obtain a commodity total. However, if the quoted prices were extended for volume, the existing supplier's total would be much higher. This supplier might not be the low bidder.

The consultant's price analysis of the 1989 bearing BOR update confirmed the presence of this pricing practice. Purchasing had fallen into a pricing trap. It officially reported a $20,000 cost savings to its management in 1989 as a result of this BOR competitive bid update. In actuality, when extended for the volume profile, Purchasing approved a $30,000 price increase without knowing it.

Clearly, this bearing Procurement Process offers the firm involved significant opportunity for improvement. The techniques outlined throughout this book are directly applicable to this bearing purchase example. The potential exists for cost savings of 30 percent and inventory reductions of over 60 percent through the development and implementation of strategic Supply Management principles.

ACQUIRING SERVICES

Services ranging from software development to advertising to janitorial services represent a gold mine of savings opportunities. Due to the complex nature of such procurements, AKT relationships frequently will be in the common interest of both the buyer and the supplier. However, these agreements are also quite challenging.

Hidden Opportunities

Warren Norquist, vice president of International Materials Management at Polaroid, has involved his staff in the following nontraditional procurements:

- Print ad production.
- General consultants.
- Computer consultants.
- Television ad production.
- Outplacement agencies.
- Training consultants.
- Network TV time.
- Market research.

- Financial auditors.
- Training courses.
- Per diem help.
- Placement agencies.
- Technical consultants.
- Spot TV and radio time.
- Annual reports.

Mr. Norquist's experience is that when qualified personnel are involved in the planning and procurement of such services, savings of 25 percent are enjoyed with equal or improved quality and service.[2]

The outsourcing of services is progressing from operational level services to activities long considered to be integral to the firm's operation and identity. For example, Commodore Business Machines, Inc., has outsourced its telephone customer service operation to Federal Express. Software giant Lotus Development Corporation has outsourced its computer network management to Digital Equipment. Samsung Electronics America, Inc., lets Design Continuum, Inc., design all of its consumer electronics products. The forklift division of Clark Equipment Co. uses Harper Group, Inc., a freight forwarder, for logistics and inventory control.[3] Such outsourcing allows the firm to focus on its core business, while simultaneously enjoying cost savings and risk minimization. The principles in *The American Keiretsu* apply to each of these outsourcing efforts.

Keys to Success When Obtaining Services

The successful procurement of services results from exactly the same process that has been outlined for production materials.

There are eight keys to success when obtaining services:

- A thorough and complete understanding of the true need.
- Research and analysis of all potential suppliers.
- Cross-functional development of the appropriate selection criteria.
- Selection of the top two or three best-qualified suppliers, based on the specific criteria.
- Joint development of the statement of work (SOW).
- Selection of *the* supplier(s).
- Refinement of the SOW and negotiation of commercial terms that motivate the supplier to meet the customer firm's needs.
- Measurement and management of performance.

Temporary Labor Example

Many firms spend a considerable amount of money for temporary help each year. At most of these firms, this activity is handled by the human resource organization, with limited involvement by Purchasing. Firms such as Manpower Temporary Services, Kelly Temporary Services, and many others specialize in providing part-time help for companies on a temporary basis. Typically, arrangements for temporary help are handled as independent events by the local human resources department.

Canada Post Corporation, however, has taken a different approach. Purchasing management at Canada Post observed that it had a history of hiring temporary help throughout Canada from dozens of service providers in support of holiday mail volumes and other mail volume related issues. Armed with five years of actual usage, cost history by location, and projections for future requirements, Canada Post management was able to develop highly attractive AKT agreements with a few Canadian suppliers able to support its needs. Significant improvements in temporary labor quality and response time, in addition to meaningful cost reductions, are now being realized.

Corporate Legal Services Example

Many COOs have expressed concern about the difficulties and expense involved in retaining outside legal counsel. Questions concerning cost—benefit analysis, billing accuracy, time charges, retainer fees, and so on, swirl around this issue at many firms. Frequently, contracting duties are assigned to the in-house counsel responsible for source selection, assignments, program management, fee negotiations, and issue resolution. The legal profession has a vested interest in this issue. Clearly, there must be a better way to retain professional services, gain the desired benefits, appropriately reward the professional involved, and leave the experience with the knowledge that the fees were appropriate.

Utilizing AKT techniques in this complex area offers firms an alternative. This approach requires knowledge and sensitivity. The potential rewards, however, are well worth the extra effort. As with other critical areas, each initiative must be well thought-out and customized for the specific situation.

The check list shown in Figure 8-3 was developed recently to assess effectiveness improvements at a Fortune 200 firm in the procurement of legal services. This process is also applicable to the procurement of recurring consulting, accounting, and audit services.

FIGURE 8–3
Project Outline

Purchasing Legal Services

Project Goals:
- Identify:
  - —Sourcing process.
  - —Selection criterion.
  - —Evaluation measures.
  - —Alternative processes.

Data Requirements:
- File search.
  - —Legal firms retained for the last five years.
  - —Dollars spent by firm by year.
  - —Services provided by firm by year.
- Internal research.
  - —Identify internal processes.
- External research.
  - —Conduct supplier survey.

Analysis Requirements:
  - —Sourcing trends.
  - —Special services required by organization.
  - —Ongoing services required by organization.
  - —Evaluate alternatives.
  - —Evaluate services provided against services costs.
  - —Research alternative approaches.
  - —Benchmark alternatives.

CONCLUDING REMARKS

The procurement of nonproduction items and services represents a gold mine of opportunities. The productivity implications of such requirements *demands* top managerial attention. Many of these requirements lend themselves to AKT relationships. However, this is a particularly challenging area that requires specialized experience and professionalism.

We now turn our attention to managing AKT relationships.

NOTES

1. C. K. Prahalad and Gary Hamel, "The Core Competence of the Corporation," *Harvard Business Review* (May–June, 1990), p. 82.
2. Burt, Norquist, and Anklesaria, *Zero Base Pricing*™: *Achieving World Class Competitiveness through Reduced All-In-Costs* (Chicago, IL: Probus Publishing Company, 1990), p. 92.
3. Anita Micossi, "Farming It Out," *Enterprise* (July 1992), p. 32.

CHAPTER 9

MANAGING AN AMERICAN KEIRETSU-TYPE RELATIONSHIP

Thou must realize that plans are only dreams without action.[1]

Og Mandino

THE LIFE CYCLE OF AN AMERICAN KEIRETSU-TYPE RELATIONSHIP

At the 1992 National Association of Purchasing Management conference, Professor Robert Monczka of Michigan State University stated that "80 percent of all partnerships end in divorce."[2] The source of Mr. Monczka's data is unknown, as is his meaning of the term *partnership*. However, this statement, along with growing empirical evidence regarding the dynamic nature of business relationships and prudent business practice, supports the need for systematic relationship planning and management. Sound planning and management will extend the life of the relationships as long as they are mutually beneficial. Specific projects, most or all of which will have a shorter life than the umbrella relationship under which they operate, make the management of the relationship challenging. When establishing the umbrella relationship, one should plan for the possible need of relationship renewal.

A variety of forces strain American Keiretsu-type (AKT) relationships: personnel reassignments, potential complacency, shifting priorities, the inherent business ebb and flow, and stresses associated with specific projects, to name a few. As such forces demand attention, the business managers at both firms must initiate joint corrective actions to get the relationship back on track. It is anticipated that the majority of issues will be resolved directly. On occasion, it may be appropriate to secure outside professional assistance to conduct an objective analysis and, possibly, to provide assistance. In extreme cases, shifting corporate priorities, senior management changes, divestiture, and acquisition activity may force an end of the relationship.

Relationship/Business Managers

Each strategic alliance requires the formal assignment of relationship managers at both firms.[a] These managers frequently are selected from Purchasing at the customer firm and marketing or operations at the selling firm; however, this is not a requirement. Other assignments are possible. These individuals assume the role of ombudsman. They provide a focal point and a clearinghouse for day-to-day issue resolution. They ensure that the strategy and the projected benefits are being measured and actively managed.

Managing the AKT relationship must be viewed as a quality management task. Every tool that has ever been developed for the improvement and maintenance of quality is applicable. Each performance problem must be viewed by both parties as a quality error. These errors must be dealt with in the same manner and with the same tools as if they were quality errors in manufacturing. In most cases, resourcing the component or service as a corrective measure to a persistent supplier problem is counterproductive. All errors, including persistent ones, must be viewed as continuous improvement opportunities by both management teams. As a matter of

---

[a]With this concept, the relationship manager is assigned by senior management based on his or her experience and competence. In the majority of cases, the individual is not an incremental resource.

fact, *if these supplier performance and relationship errors would be ranked by frequency, one would have a Pareto listing that represents a road map to excellence!*

Under traditional buyer/supplier relationships, the buyer actively monitors supplier performance in such areas as quality and delivery. As firms progress to AKT relationships, their interdependence increases. Interestingly, two major studies forecasting future manufacturing trends both identify a significant increase in interfirm dependency.[b]

After establishing a mutually beneficial AKT agreement, the customer and the supplier *must not* shift their attention to the next opportunity or challenge at the expense of the newly established relationship. Rather, both parties must manage the relationship at a strategic level and at an operational level to ensure that the anticipated technology flow, quality performance, timely availability, and the total cost of purchased materials combine to give the alliance the sustainable competitive advantage that motivated the relationship in the first place. Additionally, both parties must nurture the relationship to ensure its continued viability and growth.

Many are familiar—and perhaps frustrated—with the Japanese "ringi" process. When negotiating in Japan, it seems like everyone, including the CEO, has to sign off on a new project. (The term *ringi* describes the process of stamping the proposed agreement with one's ring, signifying acceptance.) Negotiations in Japan frequently take as much as six times as long as in the United States. However, on completion of this process, all players in the Japanese firm understand what they are to do and why the agreement is advantageous, in the present and in the long term.

The traditional American approach to deal making is faster, but considerably more naive and much less strategic. *Developing AKT relationships with suppliers is a serious strategic business.* Technology flow must be preplanned and con-

---

[b]See "2006: A Vision," which follows Chapter 10.

trolled. Source selection is strategic and critically important if the buying firm wishes to avoid contributing to the development of a new, strong competitor, one that has been funded both economically and technically through the buying firm's purchases of critical components through time.

The Philosophy of Measurement

Management without measurement is not management. AKT relationships must be held to high standards if they are to produce the joint benefits outlined in Chapter 1 on a consistent basis. Identifying, quantifying, and monitoring these standards is a key to long-term success. Traditional Purchasing and supplier performance evaluation programs fail to produce optimal results partially because the measures used do not have a high correlation with jointly desired results. Greater attention must be paid to the measurement of performance and improvement under these (and other) special relationships. Specific measures must be developed for each relationship. It is unwise to think that complex strategic supplier relationships can all be effectively managed with a generic measurement process that was designed to accommodate all suppliers across all industries, cultures, and technologies. (See Figure 9–1.)

There are six principles that drive the development of measurement philosophy. They are:

- Measures[c] must be few.
- Measures must be simple.
- The focus of a measure must *really* be important (have impact).
- Measures must be assigned to a person by name.
- Measurement status report distribution must be formalized and agreed to in advance.

---

[c]Measures are metrics specifically designed to quantify an attribute, process, or result.

FIGURE 9–1
Measurement Development and Implementation Flow Chart

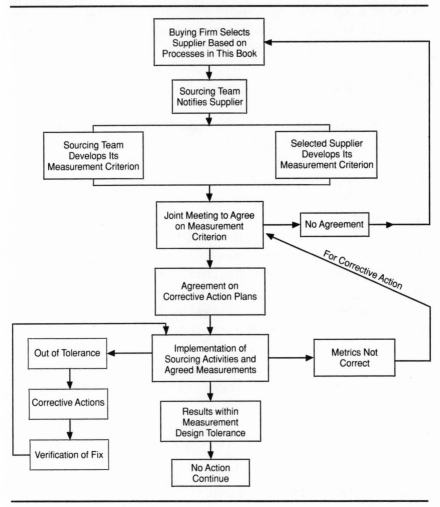

- Joint reactions to higher-lower results must be planned and agreed to in advance.

Figure 9–2 provides a partial sample of items to be measured, along with the mechanics of a measurement concept called total performance factor (TPF). This sample is taken from a measurement system for truck transportation; however, it can be adapted to most situations. It is offered only to describe this measurement technique.

FIGURE 9–2
Performance Measurement System

Truck Transportation—Total Performance Factor (TPF): Partial Example
Step One
Quality TPF:

Item	Measure
Q1	On-time factor one (on-time to request-time %)
Q2	On-time factor two (on-time to commitment-time %)
Q3	Equipment availability factor (% equipment available first call)
	(Q1%) × (Q2%) × (Q3%) = Quality TPF [Higher is Better]

Safety TPF:

S1	Claims factor (No. of claims/total hauls)
S2	Driver safety record one (No. of accidents/miles driven)
S3	Driver safety record two (traffic citations/miles driven)
	(S1%) × (S2%) × (S3%) = Safety TPF [Lower is Better]

Productivity TPF:

P1	Equipment utilization factor (utilized equipment days/total equipment days)
P2	Load productivity factor 1.0 (loaded haul) × 0.7 (empty hauls) × 0.4 (bobtail hauls)
P3	Invoices factor (% invoices electronically processed error free)
P4	Summary billing factor (% of hauls on electronic summary billing)
P5	Modern equipment factor (new equipment*/total equipment) *= <12 months in service
	(P1%) × (P2%) × (P3%) × (P4%) × (P5%) = Productivity TPF [Higher is Better]

FIGURE 9–2
Performance Measurement System (*continued*)

Carrier Competitive Measurement Summary
Step Two

TPF Trends

Quality TPF   Plot Trend
Safety TPF   Plot Trend
Productivity TPF   Plot Trend

Rate Measures

Quoted "Loaded" rates   Plot Trend
Quoted "Empty" rates   Plot Trend
Quoted "Bobtail" rates   Plot Trend

Financial Analysis

- Carrier's financial ratio trends.
- Comparison of carrier's financial position within industry.
- Expenditures per year with carrier and percent of carrier revenue.

Interfirm Teams

Interfirm contacts must be established and maintained between relevant technical groups: engineers to engineers, chemists to chemists, schedulers to schedulers, facility engineer to project manager, and so on. The dangers inherent in these interfirm teams regarding the security of technology are obvious, and these risks can only be minimized through disciplined project planning, employee training, close team supervision, and management control. Agreements governing the security of technology and establishing appropriate boundaries for cooperation must be resolved prior to technical level meetings with suppliers. As previously discussed in the section on the philosophy of measurement, formal plans must be developed, implemented, and managed to ensure the continued competitiveness of the value chain.

Progress Reviews

During the development phase of the project, frequent reviews must be conducted to ensure timely completion of the effort. Similar reviews should be scheduled to monitor progress on quality and equipment plans. Figure 9–3 shows a sample of reporting elements that may be employed at the project level.

FIGURE 9–3
Project Reporting Elements Sample

- **A program organization chart.** The supplier designates its program manager and shows the key members of the organization by name and function.
- **Milestone plan.** This plan identifies all major milestones on a time-phased basis, including those of the supplier's major suppliers.
- **Funds commitment plan.** This plan shows estimated commitments on a dollar versus time basis and on a cumulative dollar basis.
- **Labor commitment plan.** This plan shows estimated labor loading on a labor-hour versus labor-month basis.
- **Progress information.** This report should be submitted, as appropriate on joint agreement. The report should contain as a minimum:

  A narrative summary of work accomplished during the reporting period, including a technical progress update, a summary of work planned for the next reporting period, problems encountered or anticipated, corrective action taken or to be taken, and a summary of buyer-seller discussions.

  A list of all action items raised by either party.

  An update of the milestone plan showing actual progress against planned progress.

  A report on any significant changes, including personnel or any other factors that might affect performance.

  Missed milestone notification and recovery plan. Joint notification of any anticipated major milestone slip. All such anticipated difficulties require a formal recovery plan within 72 hours or sooner, as appropriate.

Coordination Meetings and Visits

Regular visits at both the managerial and operating level—ideally with the venue rotating between companies—are strongly recommended. Operating-level people, including engineering, scheduling, manufacturing, quality, and others, as appropriate, should be part of the teams or may be required to make independent visits to each other's facility. Strict focus and project discipline are required to ensure that discussions and technology reviews do not stray beyond the pre-established boundaries.

A division of a major auto manufacturer has an innovative program involving visits by factory workers. The organization invites workers from selected suppliers to come to its factories and meet with workers who are responsible for using the supplier's parts. This is done on a regularly scheduled basis. These meetings focus on quality, design, and other joint issues in an effort to find root causes and to develop corrective actions. Recently, the United Auto Workers (UAW) committee chairman and two other factory workers from a supplier visited their customer's plant. During the discussions, the root cause of an "O" ring problem was identified by the group. The UAW leader from the supplier's plant assured the customer's workers that the problem would be fixed permanently. "We can't afford to have quality problems," he said. "Our jobs are at stake." "This 'O' ring problem will be fixed; you can count on it!" These people also exchanged home phone numbers to facilitate ongoing communication.

On the downstream side, the factory workers at the customer plant also visit their customers (assembly plants) on a regular basis. Line workers from selected production departments travel (at company expense) once a month to their customers' car assembly plants and visit the assembly workers who use the parts they manufacture. At one such meeting, a car assembly employee said, "Well, your parts are OK. I don't have any problems with the parts. But the way you ship them causes me some trouble." (The parts were shipped in large reusable steel racks. Three parts were laid on their sides on the bottom of the rack and covered by a piece of cardboard. Then, three more parts were placed on their sides on top.) "What's the problem?" asked the customer production worker. "Well," said the other, "the top three parts are no problem, but when I have to reach down for the other three parts, I have to dive into the rack to reach them. Each part is a little more difficult to reach because each part is a little further away. The only way I can reach the last part at the bottom of the rack is to pull it closer by this tubing connection." (Interestingly, one of every six parts, when installed, "mysteriously" experienced a loose tubing connection.)

The parts are now shipped six parts per rack, but the parts are packed on their ends so the assembly worker no longer has to reach deep into the rack for the parts. Not only did this visit uncover the reason for a 16 percent loose tubing connection quality problem, but it greatly simplified the assembly factory worker's job. These individuals also exchanged home phone numbers so they can "stay in touch." After relaying this story, the supply manager at this facility said, "I used to have six SQA (supplier quality analysts) to try to help 300 suppliers. Now I have 1,500 factory workers from my plant and from my suppliers all working together solving quality problems."

Based on this record of success, it is highly recommended that programs in quality training include applicable American Keiretsu concepts and techniques. Such action will prepare the organization to conduct business in a new, more competitive way.

Quality Certification

Supplier-quality certification is a precondition to becoming an AKT supplier. Unfortunately, America's quality certification process is in a rather sorry state of disarray. Literally hundreds of major manufacturers impose customized certification plans on their suppliers. All too frequently, these plans are in conflict at some level.

This issue was recently emphasized by the top quality executive of a major European electronics manufacturer during an interview regarding quality certification. This executive expressed considerable frustration about the proliferation of customer-quality certification programs. He explained that his firm is currently hosting an average of three customer-quality certification audits per week. He has had to assign several quality engineers to this effort on a full-time basis. Many of these customer audit teams demand to visit multiple manufacturing facilities around the world. The electronics manufacturer must send managers to accompany these teams in an attempt to appear responsive. Often after traveling halfway around the world on such a visit, the audit team conducts its survey in a conference room and never enters the manufacturing facility. The executive estimated that this process was costing his firm over a million U.S. dollars per year. Even worse, there seems to be no end in sight.

Clearly, the above example was not the intent of these well-meaning customer-quality certification programs when they were initiated. It is recommended that firms interested in initiating supplier-quality certification programs explore this issue with their suppliers. Considerable savings and efficiency appear to be available by accepting a supplier's current quality-certification policy if it is reasonable, instead of imposing yet another formal program to accomplish the same result.

International Standards Organization (ISO) 9000[3]

The ISO 9000 standards establish requirements for quality systems in Europe. They were designed to be generic standards that would apply to all products and industries. As such, they may offer a partial solution to the duplication outlined in the previous section. The ISO 9000 series contain five standards. A broad scope of quality system elements are covered by the ISO 9000 series, including management responsibility; quality system; contract review; document control; Purchasing; process control; inspection and testing; design control; control of nonconforming products; corrective actions; handling, storage, packaging, and delivery; quality records, internal quality audits, training, and servicing.

The standards have been adopted by the European Community and by the individual nations of that community. They are being used to provide a universal framework for quality assurance. ISO 9000 is becoming a tool to ensure cross-border quality. The standards are also being adopted by NATO, the U.S. Department of Defense, the American Society for Quality Control (ASQC), and the American National Standards Institute (ANSI). In addition, at least 51 countries around the world have adopted ISO 9000.

ISO 9000 is becoming a de facto market requirement for companies that wish to do business within the European Community. Some experts believe that within five years ISO 9000 registration will be necessary for businesses to be globally competitive.

Supplier Variables Data[4]

Obtaining and analyzing supplier quality data, *including variables data*, can dramatically reduce and/or eliminate incoming inspection. Quality engineering must identify the required data and make its timely submission part of the normal operating procedures. When a part is new or the part or process has been changed, the quality data must be analyzed immediately to provide feedback to the supplier. If the supplier is certified, analyses must be conducted only when variables data are inconsistent or shifting.

Changes

The engineering change control function at each firm must be the focal point for all communication on all engineering changes. Such discipline ensures configuration, cost management, and project timing integrity.

Offspecs

At many firms, waivers or deviations of specification requirements are made on a "one-time" basis to accommodate materials that are urgently required, but which do not meet specification. Acceptance of nonconforming material sends a faulty message to suppliers and undermines quality efforts. Many firms have established a policy of "no more offspecs." At such firms, if the responsible engineer is willing to accept a nonconforming item twice, then the specification must be revised to reflect the change before the material is accepted. As a result, more realistic specifications are being developed. Frequently, these specifications result in a more manufacturable purchased item. The firm's quality culture is preserved with its suppliers. The net result is improved incoming quality at lower prices.

CONCLUDING REMARKS

Recently, the breakdown of a major collaborative relationship was witnessed. The failure by both parties to manage actively their carefully crafted agreement resulted in much anger, the departure of executives responsible for managing the agreement, and the abandonment of a significant global advantage for both firms. AKT relationships require active management and nurturing. But the rewards are well worth the effort!

We now turn our attention to the implementation of America's new strategic weapon: the American Keiretsu.

NOTES

1. Og Mandino, *The Greatest Success in the World* (New York: Bantam Books, 1981), pp. 70, 76.
2. Robert Monczka, "The Life Cycle of a Keiretsu Relationship," NAPM Conference, Orlando FL (May 4–6, 1992).
3. This section is based on Donald W. Marquardt's article: "ISO 9000: A Universal Standard of Quality," *Management Review* (January 1992), pp. 50–52.
4. Based on W. E. Norquist, "Improving Quality/Purchasing Teamwork," in *37th Annual Quality Congress Transactions* (Milwaukee, WI: A.S.Q.C., 1983), pp. 136–41.

CHAPTER 10

HOW TO GAIN THE BENEFITS OF STRATEGIC SUPPLY MANAGEMENT

Progress is agonizingly slow. But unless we begin, the task will never be done—1982:

Robert B. Stone, Vice President, Materials Management, General Motors[1]

Chapter 1 introduced and discussed the five goals of strategic supply management (see Figure 1–2) as follows:

- Continuous quality improvement.
- Management and measurement of total cost.
- Velocity—the time dimension of competition.
- Technology access and control.
- Risk identification, management, and reduction.

Upon reflection, executives overwhelmingly accept these five goals as basic core objectives in every business. Given this acceptance, one would expect to find considerable focus directed to meeting these goals through current supply (procurement) management processes at most firms. Our research provides strong evidence *that this is not the case.* Most executives are uncomfortable with their limited awareness and understanding of the firm's current supply (procurement) management process compared with other processes such as marketing, conversion, and finance. Many executives also feel they lack objective data on past effectiveness and current trends in this critical area.

The high-profile media attention focused on the General Motors purchasing function during late 1992 has caused many senior executives around the world to wonder, Do we need GM-type chemotherapy, aspirin and bed rest, or simply more exercise? This question drives to the heart of *The American Keiretsu*. Uncertainty about the current status of a firm's Supply Management process and progress toward improvement goals is unacceptable in today's global markets.

DEVELOPMENT OF THE IMPLEMENTATION PLAN

The paradigm shift from Purchasing to strategic Supply Management is every bit as—or more—significant than the transition from the sales concept (selling what the firm produces) to the marketing concept (identifying customer wants and needs and then satisfying them), as outlined by Ted Levitt in his *Harvard Business Review* classic of 1960, "Marketing Myopia."[2] It has taken all these years for the marketing concept to replace the sales concept at many firms. The frightening thing is that we do not have the luxury of 30 years to progress to strategic Supply Management—global competition will not allow a firm such a gradual transition. Even more frightening is the fact that the path to strategic Supply Management may be even more challenging. But as Spyros Makridakis writes in his book *Addressing Strategies for the 21st Century*, "Competition necessitates the formulation and implementation of appropriate strategies in order to gain competitive advantages and maintain them as long as possible."[3] In the three years since this statement was published, the geopolitical and geoeconomic changes indicate that there is considerable urgency to the formation and implementation of appropriate Supply Management strategies.

THREE APPROACHES

The authors have concluded that effective strategic Supply Management plans, including American Keiretsu-type

FIGURE 10–1
Integrated Strategy Interdependence Model

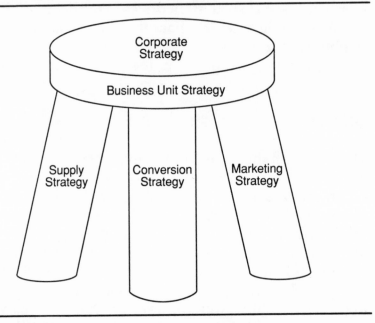

Developed by Charles L. Hinkle, Ph.D., and Michael Doyle, 1987.

(AKT) relationships, cannot be developed or implemented in a vacuum by the Purchasing or materials organization. As previously discussed, strategic Supply Management is not a simple purchasing plan, but a major subsection of the firm's strategic business plan, as shown in Figure 10–1.

There are three major procedural approaches to the development of the initial detailed strategic Supply Management implementation plan:

- An internally staffed project.
- A consulting project.
- A hybrid project.

Internally Staffed Projects

Some organizations have adopted this approach to the development of major change initiatives. The individuals involved usually find these types of projects both satisfying and highly rewarding. Senior executives often find these assignments provide outstanding opportunities for staff growth and training.

The shortcomings are that:

- Many firms do not have the luxury of reassigning critical resources for the time required to complete such complex projects.
- The organization must reinvent and discover, through trial and error, those methods and processes that produce World Class results in this strategic area, given their unique industry, position, and culture.
- Multicultural, multiindustry lessons, approaches, and learning commonly are unavailable.

Consulting Projects

Many firms frequently turn to outside consultants when confronted with critical and complex projects of the type discussed. This approach resolves the temporary assignment issue previously discussed and offers a workable solution to the extent that consultants with the appropriate professional experience can be retained. Clearly, professional consultants normally apply considerable multicultural and multiindustry experience and focus to complex projects of this type.

The shortcomings are:

- There is a significant shortage of professional consultants with the required experience, background, and training in strategic Supply Management.
- Costs can range from 25 thousand dollars to well over 10 million dollars, dependent on organization size and complexity.
- The organizational learning enjoyed through the first method is typically more limited with this approach.

- Unfortunately, the long history of successful implementation of otherwise outstanding consulting work has been less than perfect.

Hybrid Projects

The third approach incorporates the strengths of both the internally staffed project and the consulting approach. It takes advantage of outside expertise to facilitate the project and the many tasks involved, primarily using internal resources. This approach provides the retained organizational learning while keeping the consultant's focus on the facilitation role.

The shortcomings of this approach include:

- Many professional consulting firms refuse to work in this manner because these firms have learned that project controls, schedules, and budgets are more difficult to manage using client resources that are inexperienced in consulting methodology.
- The nature of consulting projects requires that all possible alternatives be analyzed and considered. Such action can create considerable and unnecessary organizational stress and, possibly, lost productivity to the extent that these considerations are available to client's middle management prematurely.

Selecting the Correct Approach

Quite obviously, there are trade-offs to be considered with each of these three approaches. The correct approach for any organization should be based on its unique history, culture, and circumstances.

GETTING STARTED

There is an old proverb: If you don't know where you're going, *any* road will get you there. This admonition would appear to be applicable for the development of an implementation plan for a new approach to any established business practice. It is definitely true with the implementation planning for strategic Supply Management. There is a corollary to this old proverb, however, that also applies: If you don't know where you are, it is difficult to get started. These twin issues (a clear vision of the objectives and a thorough understanding of current practice) represent the two major challenges to developing a strategic Supply Management implementation plan.

Organizations committed to the implementation of strategic Supply Management must first establish *a clear vision and commitment* to capture the opportunities available through a strategic approach to their upstream value chain; and, second, they must establish a thorough *baseline understanding* of the effectiveness of their current practices and process.

The first challenge has been the focus of the preceding nine chapters. The goal has been to provide the necessary vision, stimulate appropriate commitment, and drive implementation initiatives within American industry. The second major challenge is the baseline understanding and measurement of the firm's current Procurement Process and practices.

It is vitally important to note that a firm's Procurement Process includes all activities extending from the initial component design or development of the statement of work to make/buy considerations to supplier selection, invoice payment, and recycle/landfill considerations. Based on this view, one can see that the firm's Procurement Process involves many, if not most, of the firm's functional activities. The Purchasing department commonly is only one of many players in the firm's Procurement Process.

The importance of a thorough baseline understanding of the firm's Procurement Process cannot be overstated. *This process drives current and long-term results.* Strategic Supply Management and American Keiretsu-type (AKT) relationships normally cannot be institutionalized without redesigning the Procurement Process. *It is not a lack of effort of those involved in the current process that is to blame for suboptimal results; it is process itself.* Typically, the Procurement Process has evolved in a hand-me-down fashion. This process has rarely been reviewed by senior management nor has it undergone careful scrutiny, as have most of the other important processes within the firm.

A complete understanding of the complex Procurement Process generally requires the triangulation of the results of three separate analyses. This research forms the foundation of the implementation plan discussed later in this chapter. The triangulation techniques include benchmarking, process flow analysis, and the measurement and analysis of actual effectiveness trends.

Benchmarking

The concept of benchmarking involves a comparison of processes, functions, results, and so forth. These comparisons yield a listing of specific differences (gaps) between the attributes being compared. Gap analysis techniques evaluate the differences to determine their significance and potential for improvement. As shown in Figure 10-2, there are three widely used approaches to benchmarking. Each approach has its own strengths and weaknesses. The time and cost attributes are straightforward. The term *actionable* indicates whether the specified approach to benchmarking serves as the basis of action that the firm may take to improve specific Procurement Processes and practices. The term *validity* indicates the level of confidence those involved in the specific benchmarking approach have in the applicability of findings resulting from the approach. The term *thoroughness* indicates the breadth of the benchmarking approach.

The first benchmarking approach (review against standard) involves an evaluation against an ideal or "standard." This standard normally represents the "best practice" that

FIGURE 10–2
Three Common Approaches to Benchmarking

Type	Cost	Time	Actionable	Validity	Thoroughness
Review against standard	Low	Fast	Yes	?	Good
Process specific	High	Long	Yes	High credibility	Requires plan and focus
Competitive analysis	High	Long	Yes	High credibility	Challenging

Developed by Charles L. Hinkle, Ph.D., and Michael Doyle, 1987.

has been observed and/or developed through academic-type research. Identification and selection of the best practice is very much like playing best ball in golf. No single firm possesses all the "best practice" attributes. Therefore, the best practices must be selectively chosen from many firms across diverse industries.

The cost for this type of benchmarking is very low. The process can be completed in several days with actionable recommendations specifically aimed at identified opportunities. Validity has two concerns. First, this approach requires openness and candor to be most effective. Second, the research that originally drove the questionnaire (a sample of which is contained in Appendix A) will not be in perfect calibration for the individual firm, since it was developed for the general case and not the specific one. The thoroughness of this approach is quite good, however, as most areas of interest are probed.

The sample questionnaire contained in Appendix A has been the basis of several Procurement Process reviews. These reviews involved cross-functional teams, including representation from product development, Purchasing, quality, operations, and marketing. During the typical review, the client's procurement practices are compared with this best practice standard. Each deviation from these standards practices precipitates a root-cause analysis. The typical result of these reviews is the identification of 50 to 70 recommendations for changes that provide significant opportunities for improvement.

The second benchmarking approach (process specific) involves a direct comparison with selected firms. It is more narrowly focused on selected business processes of interest. Specific focus areas for comparison are identified. Preliminary analysis is conducted to identify firms throughout the world with a reputation for excellence in each process area of interest. Meetings are then scheduled with the appropriate functional managers at these targeted firms. Formal interview guides are developed to ensure that the benchmark team thoroughly investigates the processes of interest and leaves with an understanding of how these processes were developed and function (including interfunctional dynamics).[4]

The cost for this type of benchmarking will be much higher than the previous method. This approach may require extensive travel and could take several months to complete. The validity is outstanding as these visits offer the opportunity to view alternative approaches firsthand. The thoroughness is very good; however, the focus is, by definition, considerably more restricted. This benchmarking approach requires considerable preplanning.

The third benchmarking approach (competitive analysis) involves a direct comparison of selected business processes with those of the firm's competitors. This analysis yields specific data on competitive advantages and disadvantages. This approach generally involves an indirect analysis using published financial data, product data, and other information that is publicly available. These studies usually take one of two directions. In some instances, industry organizations and other professional organizations collect industrywide performance data and publish studies that allow benchmark-type analysis. The other approach involves an in-depth analysis of the industry. The focus is directed to areas of interest like purchase content percentage trends, inventory trends, supplier identification, design approaches, and so forth.

The cost for this method of benchmarking could vary, but in any event would be higher than the first method outlined. The time to complete a competitive benchmark will also vary. However, these studies commonly require several months to complete. (Some firms maintain a continuous effort in this type of competitive investigation.) The validity again is outstanding, since the results can be directly identified as competitive advantages or disadvantages. The thoroughness of this type of benchmark study is severely constrained since access to publicly available competitive data of value is normally limited.

Typically, organizations implementing strategic Supply Management utilize all three forms of benchmarking in addition to extensive supplier surveys to obtain an understanding of their relative position in the area of professionalism. We encourage this thorough approach as it provides superior data and understanding. This approach has the added benefit of increasing the number of managers having exposure to the issues and opportunities in Supply Management. This, in turn, greatly assists implementation efforts.

Process Flow Analysis

Successful implementation of strategic Supply Management requires the acceptance of a brand new paradigm involving the relationship of the firm, its suppliers, and the dynamics of value-chain economic theory. The extent of this shift in thinking very often blurs the importance of the process changes that are required and must accompany any successful implementation initiative.

Much has been written recently about implementing change within complex organizations. Of particular interest is the recent work of Robert H. Schaffer and Harvey A. Thomson: "Successful Change Programs Begin with Results," *Harvard Business Review,* January–February 1992, in which improvement efforts are compared. The authors contrast important activity-centered programs like "total quality," "continuous improvement," "interfunctional collaboration," "middle-management empowerment," and "employee involvement" with results-driven programs. Their concern that outstanding activity-centered programs not distract from (or substitute for) the competitive necessity for results seems well taken. Rosabeth Kantor (recent editor of the *Harvard Business Review*) has authored outstanding works on the subject of change management: *The Change Makers* (1983) and *The Challenge of Organizational Change* (1992). These and other works address the complexities involved in achieving and sustaining change in complex organizations.[5]

One is reminded of an old story about a sociologist who also raised and trained pigeons. Over time, the man noticed that each pigeon appeared always to sit in the exact same place. He verified this observation and decided to try to change this pattern. Each day the man would hit the pigeon coop with a hammer and the pigeons would fly off in every direction. The next day, however, each pigeon was back in its specific place. The sociologist finally realized that in order to change the sitting pattern of his pigeons, he had to reconstruct the pigeon coop itself.

There is considerable similarity between this story about pigeons and the effect of the majority of employee education and training programs. Employees are sent off to seminars to learn the latest concepts and techniques. Then they return to their place of employment only to discover that both the work processes and their colleagues require that they do everything exactly the same as before. These employees are wiser and better informed, but they are also more frustrated as they can now more clearly see the inefficiency contained within their activity-based jobs.

Strategic Supply Management implementation requires job process redesign. However, before the process can be redesigned it must be mapped and understood. Therefore, a thorough understanding of the actual Procurement Process is an essential first step. Firms generally do not understand or appreciate the complexity involved in their Procurement Process. Process mapping activity must include the entire flow from design through each step until the supplier's invoice is paid. Figures 5–3 (a), (b), and (c) (Chapter 5) provide an example. Several firms have used fishbone diagrams and/or industrial engineering techniques to develop process maps that were meaningful in their industry and culture.

Processes of interest include, but are not limited to:

- Purchase component design and/or selection.
- Engineering change activity.
- Specification development.
- Requisition development.
- Source identification.
- Bid evaluation.
- Make-or-buy analyses.
- Source selection.
- Production and maintenance planning.
- Inbound freight.
- Receiving activities.
- Invoice and payment processes.
- Scrap and waste disposal.

Analysis of Actual Effectiveness Trends

Organizations often find that there is considerable misunderstanding about their Procurement Processes and the effectiveness of these processes. Management's perception of the process is generally at odds with the working-level employee's experience: actual process input and output trends often do not support either. The firm's suppliers have a very different view of the organization's Procurement Process, and such input is essential.

The process understanding task requires that the process be mapped at four levels. First, the process should be mapped as outlined by management. Second, the process should be mapped as outlined by the people involved in it every day. Third, the firm should identify and quantify the process input and output trends. And fourth, suppliers should be surveyed (on a confidential and independent basis) for their opinions, views, and suggestions on the process. The results of these inputs and trends must be analyzed and evaluated to determine the effectiveness of current activity and to quantify opportunities for a process redesign effort.

Implementation Plan Research

The Implementation Research Flow Chart (Figure 10–3) outlines the activities of a typical strategic Supply Management effectiveness study and implementation initiative. The process begins with executive management. The organization's executive committee (chairman and/or CEO) normally sponsors and funds the initiative. In the first step, the project scope is identified and documented, goals are established, timetables are set, and specific project resources are identified and assigned.

A full-time project manager (usually a consultant) manages the day-to-day project activity. The project manager normally reports to a senior management steering committee or to the CEO. This committee includes the top operational and functional managers of the organization. The committee is responsible for the project scope, schedules, interim reporting, and access to necessary data and facilities.

The project timing, cost, and resource requirements are directly proportional to the size and complexity of the firm.

FIGURE 10-3
Implementation Research Flow Chart

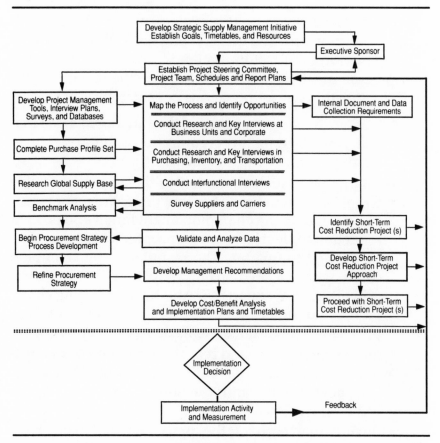

As an example, single plant firms with revenues under $50 million could expect results within two or three months, larger firms could easily require several months to years depending on their size and the scope of the project.

Project costs should not be a stumbling block. Projects of this type are typically self-funding. Actual documented project savings after 18 months, ranging from 5 to 30 times the project cost, are common.

IMPLEMENTING THE PLAN

The process of developing the implementation plan is relatively straightforward and generic compared with the process of implementing the resulting plan. Since the implementation process must be tailored to the specific situation, our guidance for this crucial process is considerably shorter:

- Assign champions in each of the functional areas that will benefit from the organization's progression to strategic Supply Management.
- Charge each such champion to develop quantifiable target benefits in his or her functional area. For example, the marketing champion might target a 50 percent reduction in development (concept to customer) time by the eighth quarter. The manufacturing champion could target a 40 percent reduction in scrap and re-work costs by quarter 6. And the purchasing champion could target a 10 percent reduction in purchase prices for 50 high-dollar items or services by quarter 4.
- Monitor, measure, and report progress on cost reductions, cost avoidances, improvements in time to market, new-product introductions based on supplier technology, and so forth.
- Ensure that each of the processes that have been mapped as part of the development of the baseline understanding (as described earlier in this chapter) are monitored to ensure continuous improvement.

CHARGE

In order to regain and maintain our global competitiveness—whether in process industries, manufacturing, or service industries, we must incorporate the benefits resulting from strategic Supply Management.

We hope that we've done our part. THE REST IS UP TO YOU!

NOTES

1. Robert B. Stone, "The Just In Time System: Its Relevance for the U.S. Auto Industry," *Industry at the Crossroads*, Michigan Papers in Japanese Studies, University of Michigan (1982).
2. Theodore Levitt, "Marketing Myopia," *Harvard Business Review* 53, no. 5 (July–August 1960), pp. 45–56.
3. Spyros G. Makridakis, *Forecasting, Planning, and Strategy for the 21st Century* (New York: The Free Press, 1990), p. 143.
4. See Michael J. Spendolini, *The Benchmarking Book* (New York: AMACOM, 1992), and Robert C. Camp, *Benchmarking: The Search for Industry Best Practices that Lead to Superior Performance* (Milwaukee, WI: Quality Press, American Society for Quality Control, 1989).
5. Rosabeth Kantor, *The Change Masters: Innovation for Productivity in the American Corporation* (New York: Simon and Schuster, 1983) and *The Challenge of Organizational Change* (New York: The Free Press, 1992).

2006: A VISION

In 1987, representatives of 10 major Japanese industries (sponsored by the Japan Machinery Federation and The Systems Sciences Institute of Waseda University, and funded through revenue from parimutuel betting at racetracks) began a five-year project to explore the future of Japanese manufacturing. This initiative, called "Manufacturing 21," addresses the following four issues:

- How to develop highly flexible "post-JIT" manufacturing.
- How to adjust the organization of human resources to respond to the new flexible manufacturing environment.
- How to develop truly integrated software systems.
- How to attract top people to follow careers in manufacturing.

In addition to identifying actions for Japanese manufacturing of the future, this formal Japanese group has offered the following advice to North American manufacturers:

Manufacturing 21 holds at least "two" important lessons for North American manufacturing. One is that if the future North American manufacturing is to be compatible to the scenario of Manufacturing 21, long-range planning and development must receive much more emphasis. Second, one company cannot work its way into such a future on its own. The new kind of manufacturing belongs to **supply chain** (emphasis added) and consortial companies.[1]

Subsequently, in 1991, over 100 American manufacturing executives, in coordination with the Department of Defense and the Iacocca Institute at Lehigh University, formulated a structured manufacturing vision and strategy and recommended a continuation mechanism to implement that strategy. This prestigious group believes that "agile manufacturing" will be in place by 2006. The group agreed that:

- A new competitive environment for industrial products and services is emerging.
- Competitive advantage will belong to agile manufacturing enterprises—ones capable of responding rapidly to demand for high-quality, highly customized products.
- Agility requires integrating flexible technologies with the skill base of a knowledgeable work force and flexible management structures that stimulate cooperative initiatives within and between firms.
- An agile enterprise has the flexibility to adopt for each project. Sometimes this will take the form of an internal cross-functional team *with participation by suppliers and customers.*

This group of American manufacturing executives believes that building the required new infrastructure will provide a unique opportunity for American industry to regain its lost industrial leadership.[2]

Interestingly, the visions of the manufacturing leaders in both America and Japan deal with a level of interfirm cooperation virtually unimaginable a few years ago. The concepts, principles, and prescriptions contained in *The American Keiretsu* are well positioned to play a crucial role in implementing the strategies recommended by these two groups. AKT relationships will become the norm, rather than the exception, in the forthcoming era of agile manufacturing.

2006: A VISION

1. *Manufacturing 21 Report* (Wheeling, IL: Association for Manufacturing Excellence, 1990), p. 2.
2. *21st Century Manufacturing Enterprise Strategy* (Bethlehem, PA: Iacocca Institute, Lehigh University, 1991), p. 7.

APPENDIX A

THE SUPPLY MANAGEMENT REVIEW

Appendix A provides an example of the types of questions that a firm may use when conducting a "best practices" benchmark, as discussed in Chapter 10. Appendix A is not intended to be all-inclusive. All of the questions will not apply to all firms. The "best practices" benchmarking questionnaire must be tailored to the specific situation. Appendix A is included since it provides a good beginning for the assessment process.

REQUIREMENTS PLANNING AND DEVELOPMENT

Technology

1. Does the firm conduct technology scans?
2. Does the individual/department responsible for such scans disseminate new technology information to marketing and engineering that may help in new-product and new-features identification?
3. Is Purchasing involved in technology access and control?

New Product Ideas

4. Are appropriate members of the cross-functional Supply Management team involved in brainstorming for new-product ideas?
5. Are appropriate members of the cross-functional

Supply Management team involved in idea and concept screening and concept scoring?

6. Are new-product designs revolutionary or evolutionary? (As a rule of thumb, incorporate a maximum of 25 percent change in any new product.)

Product Design

7. Is quality function deployment (QFD) employed when establishing design objectives?

8. Is the importance of a product feature to a customer and the customer's customers identified so that the appropriate cost benefit analysis may be conducted?

9. Are there safeguards to ensure that engineers/chemists/technologists are not driving the "state-of-the-art" unnecessarily?

10. Do appropriate members of the cross-functional Supply Management team contribute to the process of establishing price, performance, quality, and reliability objectives during the design process?

11. Do appropriate members of the cross-functional Supply Management team become involved in scheduling of time lines for new products?

12. During the design process, do appropriate members of the cross-functional Supply Management team comment on the probability of obtaining the desired level of quality of required material?

13. Are new components (compounds) *with unknown* field histories introduced into new products?

14. Are manufacturability implications of different materials considered during the design of new products?

15. During design, is consideration given to possible constraints posed by potential supplier(s) capacity?

16. Is there an active design change management program?
17. Is there an active standardization program?
18. Which of the following is *actively* considered during design?
    - Manufacturability.
    - Automated assembly.
    - Build in diagnostics.
    - Serviceability.
19. Do you take actions to limit product liability during design?
20. Are all designs subjected to value engineering techniques?
    - At each design point?
    - Before ordering materials and equipment?
21. On the typical product, how many engineering/design/chemical product changes are processed after production begins?
22. Are buyers co-located with designers (technologists)?

Quality

23. Does quality assurance review proposed design specifications and manufacturing plans to ensure that the quality called for in the marketplace is the quality that will result if engineering's design is followed?

The design of experiment (DOE) identifies the causes of variation through the use of appropriate, statistically designed experiments. DOE allows us to:

- Discover variables both in product and process design.

- Reduce drastically the variations they cause.
- Open up the tolerances on the unimportant variables so as to reduce cost.
- Identify the source of quality problems on old products.

24. Are all members of the design team aware of the impact of variation on overall quality and cost?

25. What actions are taken to reduce variation in both the end product and in its purchased components throughout the value chain?

26. Is DOE used to separate important variables from unimportant ones for both the product and the process?

27. Are environment overstress tests used to identify weak links in the design?

28. Do engineers/chemists/technologists focus on the design center (or target value) of a parameter or on specification limits and tolerances?

29. What actions are taken to avoid indiscriminate and needlessly tight tolerances?

30. Are production pilot runs conducted with hard tooling and production equipment in place and qualified purchased components?

31. Are failures at the pilot stage (and during production) rigorously analyzed to prevent repetition?

32. Do you conduct field tests before committing to full-scale production?

Specifications

33. Are appropriate members of the Supply Management team involved in protocol development (product specs from a benefits point of view, not a technical point of view)?

34. When developing or adopting purchase descriptions, are restrictive features that would limit competition avoided?
35. Is procurement research employed to investigate the availability of commercial products before employing unique design specification?
36. Are critical parameters (as identified through DOE) identified on drawings and/or specifications?
37. Are appropriate members of the Supply Management team involved in the development of technical specifications?
38. Is reliability (mean time between failures) an element of all applicable specifications?
39. Do you use a team concept when adapting specifications for purchased materials?
40. Do you involve suppliers to assist you in developing specifications?
41. Do your suppliers frequently require further clarification regarding your specifications for purchased materials?
42. Are actions taken to ensure that we do not blindly rely on previous component drawings, specifications, formulae, or supplier specifications?
43. Does your organization maintain and employ a current inventory catalog of approved materials?
44. Are performance "envelopes" used in lieu of detailed specifications for new designs whenever possible?

Suppliers

45. Are suppliers who are invited to participate in the development of new products carefully preselected by the appropriate cross-functional sourcing team?
46. Are suppliers invited to comment on the producibility of materials during the design process?

47. Are actions taken to ensure that you and your key suppliers have the required test equipment available when needed?
48. Are suppliers required to develop and submit their quality plans when developing materials, chemicals, and subassemblies for you?
49. Is Purchasing provided with advanced information on new requirements so that it may develop adequate competition?

Scheduling

50. Are sales-force estimates a reliable basis for production plans?
51. Does marketing provide realistic planning lead time for changes in demand?
52. Are two or more forecasting techniques employed in an effort to develop realistic forecasts? If yes, which ones?
53. If a materials requirements planning (MRP) system is employed, are the delivery lead times contained in the inventory status records realistic? Updated?
54. Are future anticipated prices and availabilities of required materials considered when determining inventory levels?
55. Are appropriate members of the Supply Management team aware of the following factors:
    • Suppliers' channels?
    • Raw material expiration dates (obsolescence, spoilage, etc.)?
    • Raw materials commitments?
    • Inventory carrying costs?
    • Warehouse space needs?
    • Sales forecasts?
    • Changes in product mix?

Services

56. Do you settle for vague agreements on the output of service agreements?

57. Does the internal customer or the supplier (contractor) propose the contract terms?

58. Do the internal customer and buyer collaborate to develop a procurement strategy?

59. Do you identify the qualifications required of services sources?

60. The most critical ingredient for a successful complex services procurement is the development of the statement of work (SOW). The SOW identifies what the supplier is to accomplish. The clarity, accuracy, and completeness of the SOW determines, to a large degree, whether the objectives of the contract will be achieved. Does your SOW:
    - Identify the primary and subordinate objectives clearly so that both the buyer and seller know where to place their emphasis?
    - Avoid being so narrow that it stifles the supplier's creative efforts?
    - Become so broad that firms may not respond because of the risk of uncertainty involved, the inability to relate work requirements to their talents and capabilities, or because of pricing difficulties?
    - Consider administration of the resulting contract?
    - Come across so clearly that more than one interpretation is virtually impossible?

61. Do you employ early supplier involvement in the development of your SOW?

62. When planning a SOW, are the following considered:
    - Objectives of the project?

- Where the objectives originated?
- What is the current status (resource and schedule constraints) of the effort?
- Risk involved in meeting the objectives?
- What the resource, schedule, and compensation constraints are?
- What internal customer and supplier participation is needed?
- Challenging the sequencing and interrelationships of the tasks?
- Identifying supplier delivery requirements (schedule, type, quantity)?
- Identifying technical data?
- Inspection requirements?

63. Once developed, are SOW requirements challenged in these areas:
    - Why is the task needed?
    - How much does the task cost in terms of technical effort?
    - Does it contribute tangible benefits?
    - Is the value added worth the cost?
    - Is there another way to accomplish the task?
    - What would be the effect on the project if the task were deleted?

64. When buying services, do you require:
    - Written specifications?
    - Detailed analysis of costs?
    - Breakdown of billing charges?

65. Do you pay special attention in the SOW or in the terms and conditions to the:
    - Performance plan?
    - Personnel plan?
    - Environmental factors?

- Administrative factors including contract award procedures, time required for proposal evaluation and award, liability insurance, and bonding requirements?
- Termination?
- Program organization chart?
- Milestone plan?
- Funds commitment plan?
- Labor commitment plan?
- Progress information?
- List of all action items?
- Milestone plan update showing actual versus planned progress?
- Funds commitment plan update showing actual versus planned progress?
- Significant changes report?
- Missed milestone notification and recovery plan?

Plant and Equipment

66. Is the Supply Management team involved at the earliest stage of construction requirements?
67. Is consideration given to the various methods of obtaining construction?
68. How is productivity addressed during the determination of plant and equipment requirements?
69. When developing purchase descriptions for capital equipment, is action taken to ensure that the description is precise enough to satisfy the organization's needs (technical, delivery, price information, and availability) without unduly restricting competition?
70. If equipment specifications are developed under contract, does the customer firm obtain title to the resulting data?

71. When developing requirements for capital equipment, are performance specifications considered and used, when appropriate?

72. When the firm is developing capital equipment requirements, is Purchasing responsive to its customers' needs for technical, delivery, and price information on available products?

73. When purchasing equipment, does the Supply Management team ensure that:

   - Alternative suppliers are considered?
   - Payment terms are appropriate?
   - Performance requirements are included in the warranty?
   - There is proper and adequate sourcing for accessories?
   - There is a reasonable cancelation clause that establishes commitment costs at each milestone?
   - Installation costs are included?
   - Equipment is compatible?
   - There is initial and follow-up training?
   - Who is responsible for and who pays for maintenance?
   - Who supplies and replenishes repair parts and kits?
   - Who has ownership and liability during shipping?

74. When purchasing capital equipment, does Supply Management:

   - Coordinate with all appropriate functional areas in dealing with suppliers?
   - Obtain and consolidate required information?
   - Maintain competition?
   - Address terms and conditions?
   - Address price (total cost of ownership)?

- Address spares and services?
- Address warranty by OEMs (original equipment manufacturer)?
- Address management of the resulting contract?
- Address ownership of design or intellectual properties?

75. When addressing terms and conditions in the request for proposal and resulting contract for equipment, do you include:

- Payment terms?
- Performance standards?
- Inspection procedures?
- Warranties against defects?
- A performance warranty?
- Supplier responsibility for post-sale services?
- Indemnity for patent infringement?
- Operator training responsibility?
- Installation responsibility?
- The extent of liability for employee accident?

SOURCING

Teams

1. For critical materials and services, is sourcing a cross-functional team activity?

Technology

2. Does your technology road map impact on your sourcing actions?

Make-or-Buy

3. Is the Supply Management team involved in make-or-buy analysis?
4. When performing a make-or-buy analysis, do you consider:
   - Your core technology?
   - All relevant costs?
   - Availability?
   - Control of production?
   - Quality?
   - Composite effect on firm's total operation?
5. Is a make-or-buy analysis conducted on all significant components of new products?
6. Are make-or-buy analyses conducted before a decision is made to perform a service in-house or to obtain it under contract?
7. Are make-or-buy decisions reviewed periodically?

Source Selection

8. When competitive bidding is employed, is award made to the low bidder without further *price* negotiations?
9. Are potential suppliers prequalified before being invited to bid, quote, or submit proposals?
10. Are sufficient potential suppliers invited to bid, quote, or submit proposals to ensure competition?
11. Are preaward surveys conducted when purchasing items or services critical to the firm's well-being?
12. Are appropriate members of the Supply Management team involved in preaward surveys?
13. When developing a list of potential suppliers of equipment, is consideration given to the services re-

quired (delivery, maintenance support, technical advice, etc.) now and in the future?

14. In selecting suppliers, do you refer to your supply strategy? Then, do you evaluate the potential supplier's:
    - Annual sales history?
    - Key financial ratios?
    - Referral customers?
    - Size of company (employee/physical)?
    - Production defect rate?
    - Use of DOE and statistical process control?
    - Facilities?
    - Manufacturing equipment and processes?
    - Quality?
    - ISO 9000 registered (and other customer certifications)?
    - Packaging and shipping facilities?
    - Key management?

15. Will this procurement result in your becoming more than 20 percent of the supplier's business?

16. Do you develop component strategies for critical materials that drive sourcing?

17. Do you require your suppliers to demonstrate just-in-time capability?

18. Are critical suppliers within close physical proximity?

19. Are foreign sources invited to bid when appropriate?

20. If you use a foreign source, is it for:
    a. Quality of materials/service?
    b. Lower cost?
    c. Better timeliness of delivery?
    d. Better technology?

    e. Other _____?

21. When considering a purchase from a foreign source, are the following addressed:
    - Protection of core technologies and competencies?
    - Transportation time and costs?
    - Insurance?
    - Travel and administrative costs?
    - Capital tied up under advanced payments or letters of credit?
    - Buffer stocks?
    - The implications of political and economic uncertainty?

22. Do you use negotiations as the basis of source selection for complex procurements?

Supplier Relations

23. Does a sound supplier-development program exist? Describe it.

24. Do policies exist to ensure that potential suppliers are treated with courtesy and respect?

25. Does the firm have an aggressive program to progress from adversarial relations with its suppliers to collaborative ones and to AKT relationships, when appropriate?

26. Do you update your supplier base records on a quarterly basis?

27. Do you have a supplier rating system? If so, briefly describe. How does this program affect the supplier's future business?

28. Do you have an active supplier-certification program? Describe.

29. Does Supply Management periodically analyze its suppliers' ability to meet the firm's long-term needs?

30. If present suppliers appear to be unlikely to be able to meet future requirements, is timely action taken to develop the required capability?

31. Do good communications exist between Purchasing and its suppliers so that important information (new products, potential price changes, capacity, etc.) that impacts the supply strategy is obtained in a timely manner?

32. How do you ensure that a potential supply partner is World Class or has the potential of becoming World Class?

33. What is top management's involvement in your AKT alliance program?

34. Do you conduct regular, independent, confidential supplier surveys of how you are as a customer?

Standards of Conduct

35. Have standards of conduct been established and communicated to all personnel in the firm having a role in the Supply Management process (include Purchasing, design, production, and inspection personnel)?

Services

36. Who buys:
    - Financial auditors?
    - Training courses?
    - Computer consultants?
    - Per diem help?
    - Ad development and production?
    - Placement agencies?
    - Outplacement agencies?

- Consultants?
- Media time/space?
- Annual reports?
- Market research?
- Other services? _____

37. When selecting a source to perform services, is the focus on the internal customer's primary needs?

38. Are purchase orders and contracts for services structured to motivate the supplier to concentrate on the internal customer's primary needs?

39. When buying services, the internal customer may want to use a particular supplier. In such a situation, is the customer asked for a detailed justification showing why this supplier should be considered as the only source?

40. During source selection, is emphasis placed on the *total* cost and *total* benefits to the organization?

41. In addition to the traditional concerns with a prospective supplier's financial strength, management experience, and reputation, do the potential suppliers of technical services receive special analysis?

Equipment

42. When requesting quotations for equipment, does the purchasing firm establish that its terms and conditions will govern in any resulting purchase order?

43. Do requests for quotations for equipment include (as separate items) prices for periodic and emergency maintenance, repairs, and spare parts?

44. When purchasing capital equipment, is a strong warranty clause included in the contract?

45. When selecting the supplier of capital equipment, are factors such as the reliability of the prospective

seller, willingness and ability to provide required technical assistance, ability to perform required repairs quickly, the timely availability of spare parts, and the seller's service history considered?

COST MANAGEMENT

All-in-Costs (Total Costs of Purchasing and Converting Materials)

1. Are all-in-costs the basis of price comparisons?
2. Does your management information system identify the following:
   - Applicable costs associated with processing purchased materials?
   - Conversion costs?
   - Process yield loss costs?
   - Re-work costs?
   - Scrap costs?
   - Field service costs?
   - The cost of lost sales resulting from poor-quality image?

Freight

3. Are the cost and service implications of alternate shipping methods considered when making awards?
4. Are premium freight costs measured? Reported?

Price Analysis

5. Do buyers attempt to obtain a reasonable degree of competition to establish a fair and reasonable price?

6. Is a price analysis conducted on all purchases?
7. Is a determination made that the price is fair and reasonable prior to award of all orders?
8. Are accurate engineered cost estimates available for price and for cost analysis?

Cost Analysis

9. Are negotiations employed when appropriate?
10. Is cost analysis conducted when price analysis is inadequate?
11. When it is anticipated that cost analysis and/or negotiations may be required, does the request for quotations require a detailed cost estimate in support of the bid or proposal?
12. Under the foregoing conditions and also when other than a firm fixed-price method of compensation will be used, is the right of access to the prospective supplier's records established in the request for quotation and resulting contract?
13. Does profit vary with:
    a. The amount of risk?
    b. The supplier's reliability?
    c. The amount of technical input and innovation?
    d. The size of the order?
    e. Current supply and demand pattern?
14. Are target objectives and ranges of acceptable outcomes established on all critical issues prior to face-to-face negotiations?
15. When conducting cost analysis:
    • Is learning applied to both labor and materials, when appropriate?
    • Are indirect costs carefully analyzed for reasonableness?

- Is the allocation of overhead costs carefully analyzed and negotiated?
- Are general and administrative costs carefully analyzed?
- When negotiating with supply partners, is the objective to "split the profit pie" or to squeeze cost out of the partnership?

16. Do you perform a break-even analysis of your supplier's costs to improve the price of your purchased materials and services?

17. Are cost models developed and used when appropriate?

18. When negotiating for additional quantities of an item or service, are incremental costs the basis of the resulting price?

19. Do you work with your suppliers so as to understand when they recover their initial research and development investment?

20. Does your pricing recognize that a mature product demands less general and administrative expense, and no or low research and development costs?

21. Does your company accept material costs without supporting evidence?

22. How do you deal with uncertainty concerning the amount of effort that will be required by a potential supplier?

Negotiations

23. Is adequate preparation made for successful negotiations including:
    - Gaining of an understanding of the technical and production implications of the item or service?
    - Cost and price data?

- An analysis of the buyer's and the seller's strengths and weaknesses?

24. Are realistic objectives established prior to face-to-face negotiations?

25. Does the negotiating team understand the potential supplier's costs as well as the supplier's representatives?

26. Are *all* negotiators adequately trained in the use of constructive negotiating tactics?

27. Are sound tactics employed to achieve joint objectives?

28. Is Purchasing qualified to structure other than firm fixed-price contracts?

29. Is a detailed memorandum of each negotiation written and included in the contract file?

Cost Management

30. Do you require suppliers to use value analysis on the purchased materials and services to help reduce their costs and the price?

31. Do you work with your suppliers to resist and change the forces that lead to increases in supplier costs?

32. What is your company's strategy for handling price increase requests from your suppliers? From their suppliers?

33. Does your company work to reduce scrap and re-work so as to reduce material and labor costs and to increase productivity? Do your suppliers?

34. Do you use statistical process control techniques to reduce waste? Do your suppliers?

35. Does your Procurement Process function in a way that your company can benefit from volume price breaks?

Services

36. When buying services, are statements on overall price used as a benchmark to track performance?
37. Is acceptability of the price for services based on whether it is within the amount budget?
38. Do you solicit prices for recurring services every two or three years?
39. Is the price of service contracts tailored to motivate the supplier to satisfy the organization's principal objective?

Equipment

40. Is a life-cycle cost analysis the basis of total cost comparison?
41. Do you price follow-on services and support *when pricing the equipment*?

MANAGING FOR RESULTS

Planning

1. Is administration of the resulting purchase order/ subcontract properly planned and prepared for (including necessary language) in the request for quotations and resulting orders or subcontracts?
2. Is the right to data required for purchase order or subcontract administration established in the request for quotations and resulting orders?
3. When purchase orders or subcontracts are issued, is a determination made that routine or special subcontract administration is required?

4. Is a decision on the degree of quality inspection required made on each order or contract?

5. Does your firm work with quality, marketing, production planning, and top management to create an awareness of the rate at which suppliers can adjust their production without compromising quality?

6. Do you take actions to minimize hazardous waste problems at your suppliers' and their suppliers' plants?

7. Do you ever require a phased production schedule showing the time required for the operating cycle (planning, design, Purchasing, hiring, training, performance, quality monitoring, and so on)?

8. Do you require reports showing the supplier's actual and forecasted progress compared with the contract schedule, delay factors if any, and so forth?

9. Does the report contain narrative sections in which the contractor explains difficulties?

10. Is Supply Management actively involved in the corporate planning process?

11. Does Supply Management receive input and take timely action based on the firm's long-range plans?

12. Does Supply Management provide those responsible for long-range planning input in the areas of strategic opportunities arising from new materials, products, and technology; anticipated shortages; and anticipated price increases?

Communications and Feedback

13. In situations where the supplier's production *flows* into the purchaser's ongoing manufacturing operation, does an integrated communications system exist?

14. Do you have a system to provide timely feedback (both positive and negative) to your suppliers?
15. Does your feedback system address:
    a. Quality?
    b. Responsiveness?
    c. Dependability?
    d. Cost?
    e. Technology?
16. Do your suppliers warn you in advance about delays in material deliveries or other problems?
17. Do you conduct preproduction conferences to ensure complete understanding of *all* requirements and procedures?
18. Do you take proactive actions to eliminate schedule surprises?

Quality

19. Do you actively monitor all incoming quality and/or variables data?
20. Are you taking action to replace incoming inspection with certification by the supplier in conjunction with capability data?
21. When quality deviations are noted, do you and the supplier take action to eliminate the *cause* of the problem?
22. Do you review and approve your suppliers' design, production, and quality systems? If so, do you conduct incoming inspections?
23. Do you have a quality-certification process for suppliers?
24. Are you ISO registered?
25. Are your key suppliers ISO registered?

26. Do you obtain and monitor your supplier's process and quality data?
27. Have you worked with your suppliers and your internal customers to establish firm (unalterable) schedules for fixed periods (e.g., one month)?

Cost

28. Do you work with your suppliers to jointly reduce costs?

Just-in-Time (JIT)

29. Do you have the internal discipline to benefit from JIT?
30. Do you have true JIT suppliers?

Services

31. When the dollar magnitude, complexity, or criticality of the service dictates, do you conduct a pre-work meeting with the prospective supplier before awarding the contract? If so, do you review:
    - Invoicing and payment provisions?
    - Terms and conditions?
    - Schedule?
    - Staffing and supervision?
    - Site conditions, work rules, and safety?
    - Invoicing procedures and documentation (for incentive and cost contracts)?
    - Material purchase procedures (for incentive, cost, and time and materials contracts)?
    - Background checks and security clearances?
    - Insurance certificates and permits?

- Possible conflicts with other work?
- Submission of time sheets (for cost and time and materials contracts)?
- Buyer responsibilities (tools, equipment, facilities; timeliness of buyer reviews, approvals, reports, plans, and specifications)?

32. Is the relationship manager present when the project manager discusses possible changes in the original SOW, specification, or schedule with the supplier?

33. When changes are necessary, is a new price negotiated and agreed to prior to an agreement to implement the necessary changes?

34. Are your supplier inspectors:
- Carefully selected?
- Briefed by the buyer on their responsibilities, authority, and legal implications of their dealings with the supplier and the supplier's personnel?

35. Are field visits made periodically to monitor progress and to minimize the possibility of inspectors abusing their authority?

Training

36. Do you provide your suppliers with training in the following areas:
   a. Design of experiments (DOE)?
   b. Statistical process control (SPC)?
   c. Just-in-time (JIT)?
   d. Constant improvement (Kaizen)?
   e. Supply Management?
   f. Process capability analysis?

37. Do you ensure that your suppliers provide the above training to their suppliers?

Motivation

38. What do you do to motivate your key suppliers to "get even better"?
39. Do you hold supplier-quality awareness days? Supplier appreciation days?
40. Do you actively solicit feedback from your suppliers (through an objective third party) on how you are as a customer?
41. Do you publicly recognize your superior suppliers?

STRATEGIC SUPPLY ALLIANCE ISSUES

1. Do marketing and Supply Management both develop strategic alliances based on open books (cost, schedules, etc.)?
2. Do marketing and Supply Management both see members of the firm's value chain/channel as partners/competitors? or both?
3. Does management understand Supply Management's role in:
   - Total quality (the source of 50 percent of quality problems)?
   - Time-to-market (a potential savings of 15 percent to 40 percent in time-to-market)?
   - Obtaining technology from the supply world?
   - Reducing cost of goods sold (5 percent to 20 percent)?
   - Ensuring continuity of supply at attractive prices?
4. Is the Supply Management function seen as equal to marketing, operations, R&D, and finance at both the operational and strategic levels?
5. Does the firm avoid inappropriate concentrations of business with any one:

- Supplier?
- Customer?

6. Does the firm address salvage, recycling, and disposal of its products and packaging during the initial design stage?

7. Is the desired level of quality designed and built into initial prototypes and the first product sold?

8. Do members of the design team (design engineering, operations, Purchasing, and quality) visit supplier facilities to better understand supplier engineering and process capabilities, plans, and activities?

9. Do key supplier personnel visit the buying firm's operations?

10. Does the buying firm have and employ a supplier certification program on all key suppliers?

11. Do members of the firm's supply (or commodity) management teams meet with key suppliers on a regularly scheduled basis to discuss overall performance?

12. When an incoming defect is detected, is the supplier required to develop, implement, and notify the customer firm of its formal corrective action plans?

13. Are specific formal actions taken to drive costs out of the value chain?

14. Are actions taken to protect core technologies and processes, whether developed internally or acquired through carefully crafted strategic supplier agreements?

15. Does the supply system proactively monitor the external environment for innovations that may be useful in existing or new products?

16. What supply environment information do you need to ensure that your selected supply strategies are successful?

17. What supply strategies are being applied by your competition?
18. How are exploitable opportunities in the firm's supply market identified?
19. How are exploitable threats in the firm's supply market identified?
20. Can you identify advantages in collaborating with other buyers in your industry?
21. What changes in the supply marketplace appear likely?
22. How do you identify supply strategies from other industries that might be applicable to your needs?
23. Do you monitor your supplier's key people to track their movement within their company or industry?
24. Are your key suppliers monitoring their key suppliers? How do you know?
25. How do you identify shrinking supply markets?
26. Would your company benefit from a supply environment research function?
27. If "yes," what obstacles are blocking the formation of this function?
28. How would Purchasing and engineering share or allocate this responsibility?
29. Are there incentives within your company to encourage buyers to keep up-to-date with their supply environment?
30. Do you monitor your supply environment regularly?
31. Is Supply Management integrated within the corporate or SBU strategic development process to ensure compatibility of objectives and strategies?
32. Has the organization identified its strategic components and commodities?
33. Has it developed strategic component and commodity strategies that ensure continuous access to the

critical input component (or service) in an optimum, long-term, advantageous way?

34. Has the firm developed information systems that adequately meet the needs of the Supply Management system (e.g., the cost of re-work, process yield loss, scrap, field failure attributable to defects in incoming materials)?

35. Has the firm developed and implemented supply base and strategic alliance plans?

36. Does Supply Management operate in a cross-functional mode (e.g., R&D, process engineering, quality, marketing, Purchasing, etc.)?

37. Does the firm have strategic supply alliances wherein it and its suppliers share long-term objectives in areas of interdependency?

38. Do these shared objectives result in appropriate commitments in such areas as R&D, capital investment, process improvement, and so forth?

39. Do both parties work at understanding issues that arise from the other party's point of view?

40. Do *all* members of the firm recognize that they need key suppliers as much as the suppliers need them?

41. Are disciplines in place to ensure that "special" relationships stay focused and do not flow over into product or technical activities that are beyond the scope of agreed cooperation?

42. In these special relationships, has communication been planned for and facilitated through the establishment of tight operating linkages?

43. In areas of agreed cooperation, is relevant information on forecasted changes in demand, plans to discontinue a product line, technology advances, supply threats, cost data, and so forth, shared with the alliance partner?

44. Is co-location of personnel practiced?
45. Are key relationships managed and nurtured?
46. Does top management play an active role in consummating and nurturing strategic supply relationships?
47. Have current Procurement Processes been mapped (qualitatively and quantitatively)?
48. Are current Supply Management processes (including the product development process, sourcing process, pricing process, post-award process, invoicing processing, and inbound freight patterns and process) *benchmarked* periodically?
49. Has Purchasing been process-engineered to ensure that the functions it performs add value?
50. Do senior buyers possess the technical expertise to deal both with internal customers and suppliers?
51. Has the Procurement Process been reviewed to reduce or eliminate nonessential paperwork?
52. Are the parties to an AKT relationship involved in the following joint activities:
    - Production and efficiency improvement planning?
    - New-product development/component design coordination?
    - The rationalization of manufacturing, test, and logistics resources?
    - Cost management and control efforts?
    - Constant process, product, and logistics improvement?
53. Does the Supply Management team measure, document, and report the benefits flowing from its supply initiatives?
54. Does the firm have a current technology road map for strategic components and commodity classes?

55. Does the firm practice technology convergence with its AKT suppliers?

56. When the firm identifies (or estimates) R&D dollars involved in a strategic procurement, does it obtain a voice (at the supplier) in how these dollars will be invested?

57. Are there formal agreements with suppliers on intellectual property rights? (Note: This issue applies to all manufacturing and service firms, not only "high-tech" ones!)

58. Are these agreements monitored/managed to ensure that the buying firm is not paying to develop future competitors?

59. Does the firm measure total cost (or is it distracted by purchase price variance reports, price levels, and other *partial* cost reporting data)?

60. Have cost accounting practices been established that automatically set purchase prices?

61. Are the long-term business intentions of each potential strategic supplier identified (in an effort to avoid supply shocks and avoid creating competitors)?

62. Are specific actions taken to ensure that the AKT supplier's prices remain competitive?

63. Are there activity records, which provide sourcing patterns, pricing history, inventory activity, and inbound freight data for five or more years?

64. Are suppliers selected based on a strategic criterion developed through cross-functional action?

65. Does the firm map the criticality of its purchases against the *mutual* value of the supply relationship to identify time bombs?

66. Do the firm's engineers rely on its suppliers to design nonstrategic components?

67. When establishing potentially long-term supply re-

lationships, is the possibility of relationship renewal planned for? (Personnel reassignments, complacency, shifting priorities, etc., all introduce stresses that make such action desirable.)

68. Does each strategic supply alliance require the assignment of a relationship manager *by each party*?

69. Are supplier performance and relationship errors ranked by frequency? (Such action will yield a Pareto listing that represents a road map to excellence!)

70. Are strategic supply alliances managed at *both* a strategic and an operational level?

71. Are performance and improvement measured against specifically designed (relevant) metrics?

72. Are such measures assigned to a person by name?

73. Are joint reactions to out-of-tolerance results planned in advance?

74. During the development phase of a project under an AKT relationship, are frequent joint reviews conducted?

75. Are appropriate AKT supplier reporting plans implemented? (Note: See Figure 9–3.)

76. Has the firm joined with other key supplier customers to develop a common quality-certification process/plan?

INDEX

Other books of interest to you from Business One Irwin . . .

GLOBAL QUALITY
A Synthesis of the World's Best Management Methods
Richard Tabor Greene

Copublished by ASQC Quality Press/Business One Irwin

This is a complete guide for managing and coordinating different quality systems simultaneously. Greene includes 20 surefire approaches for improving quality and remaining competitive, seven *new* total-quality methods being tested in Japan, and much more! (275 pages) ISBN: 1-55623-915-7

BENCHMARKING GLOBAL MANUFACTURING
Understanding International Suppliers, Customers, and Competitors
Jeffrey G. Miller, Arnoud De Meyer, and Jinichiro Nakane

The Business One Irwin/APICS Series in Production Management

Discover what is working in the manufacturing industry, what isn't, and why. Unlike other benchmarking guides, this one has already gathered the industry statistics you need—so you won't have to! Also includes a unique benchmarking toolkit—proven effective in over 100 global corporations—that guides you through the essential steps of this quality-enhancing process. (443 pages) ISBN: 1-55623-674-3

GLOBAL PURCHASING
How to Buy Goods and Services in Foreign Markets
Thomas K. Hickman and William M. Hickman, Jr.

The Business One Irwin/APICS Series in Production Management

Locate and evaluate foreign suppliers, negotiate the purchase of foreign goods and services, arrange for shipment, and more—for maximum profitability and minimal risk! *Global Purchasing* helps you identify opportunities and buy with confidence, even if you have little or no international purchasing experience. (237 pages) ISBN: 1-55623-416-3

PURCHASING STRATEGIES FOR TOTAL QUALITY
A Guide to Achieving Continuous Improvement
Greg Hutchins

The Business One Irwin/APICS Series in Production Management

Hutchins gives you the tools to assess goods and services for quality, improve quality within your firm, and respond promptly to customer demands. You'll find real-life strategies for ensuring that your suppliers are on your team . . . know their roles . . . and strive for the same goal—total quality and customer satisfaction. (200 pages) ISBN: 1-55623-380-9

Available at fine bookstores and libraries everywhere.